LEMONS AND LIMES

LEMONS AND LIMES

75 bright and zesty ways to enjoy cooking with citrus

Ursula Ferrigno

Photography by Clare Winfield

RYLAND PETERS & SMALL
LONDON • NEW YORK

For my Italian family, for instilling the value and beauty of citrus at a very young age. Thank you for discussing, arguing and sharing your knowledge and passion for this magnificent ingredient.

Senior designer *Sonya Nathoo*
Editors *Alice Sambrook, Miriam Catley and Gillian Haslam*
Production manager *Gordana Simakovic*
Art director *Leslie Harrington*
Editorial director *Julia Charles*
Publisher *Cindy Richards*

Food stylists *Emily Jonzen and Matthew Ford*
Prop stylists *Jo Harris*
Indexer *Vanessa Bird*

First published in 2017.
This edition published in 2020 by
Ryland Peters & Small
20–21 Jockey's Fields, London WC1R 4BW
and
341 E 116th St, New York NY 10029
www.rylandpeters.com

10 9 8 7 6 5 4 3 2 1

Text copyright © Ursula Ferrigno 2017, 2020 (feature essays written by Rachel Rowley of Ballintaggart Farm www.ballintaggart.com)
Design and photographs copyright © Ryland Peters & Small 2017, 2020
ISBN: 978-1-78879-200-4
Printed in China

A CIP record for this book is available from the British Library.

US Library of Congress Cataloging-in-Publication Data has been applied for.

Notes:

• Both British (Metric) and American (Imperial plus US cups) measurements are included in these recipes for convenience; however it is important to work with one set of measurements and not alternate between the two within a recipe.

• All spoon measurements are level unless otherwise specified.

• All eggs are large (UK) or extra-large (US), unless specified as large, in which case US extra-large should be used. Uncooked or partially cooked eggs should not be served to the very old, frail, young children, pregnant women or those with compromised immune systems.

• Ovens should be preheated to the specified temperatures. We recommend using an oven thermometer. If using a fan-assisted oven, adjust temperatures according to the manufacturer's instructions.

• When a recipe calls for the grated zest of citrus fruit, buy unwaxed fruit and wash well before using. If you can only find treated fruit, scrub well in warm soapy water before using.

• Always use sterilized jars. For more information visit the Food Standards Agency (FSA) website in the UK or the United States Department of Agriculture (USDA) website in the US.

CONTENTS

INTRODUCTION

Lemons and limes are two of the most irreplaceable and intriguing, yet humble ingredients in the culinary world. They have the ability to coax out the natural highlights in virtually any type of food and make it sing on the palate. They are exceptionally healthy, rich in vitamin C, with a beautiful decorative colour and fragrance. They are also useful for seasoning, cleansing, pickling and in the making of jams and marmalades and home-made cheese and to prevent discolouration of fruits and vegetables. This book is my celebration of these wonderful, versatile fruits.

I have taken inspiration from the many classic recipes all over the world that utilize lemons and limes as a key ingredient. You will be hard pushed to find a culture that doesn't feature their presence in some form or another. Whether in classic French salad dressings, the 'cooking' by marination of raw fish in the South American ceviche, adding tang and body in preserved form to Moroccan dishes, the key sour element to fragrant Thai broths, or making a pungent and hot Indian pickle. They bring inimitable flavour to the British favourite lemon meringue pie, and to the equally famous American Key lime pie.

Along with such classics, I have added some of my own new creations for you to try. There are so many foods that marry well with the flavour of both fruits that I found it hard to whittle down the number of dishes you see within these pages! From fresh seafood to vegetables, and even sweet, buttery desserts, their addition creates effortlessly delicious food. You will find that they elevate your dishes to a higher standard of cooking. A supply of fresh lemons and limes is something no proud home-cook should be without.

On a personal note, this book has been a joy to write, particularly because lemons are an important part of my heritage. My Italian ancestors first travelled to England on a mission to sell the citrus fruit to London bars for use in highly fashionable gin and tonic cocktails. The venture was a great success and the family business grew from these humble origins into a larger business selling all kinds of fruit and vegetables.

I was raised on the Amalfi Coast in Italy, famous for its beautiful, fresh Mediterranean food and sun-drenched lemon groves. Two of the most famous varieties of lemon – the Sfusato Amalfitano and the Limone di Sorrento – are both grown along the Amalfi Coast and Sorrento, and on the island of Capri, where groves of the most fragrant lemons cling to the cliffs. Hence, I grew up cooking with these wonderful ingredients. Wrapped in a vibrantly colourful peel, their flavour has a sort of timeless aristocratic elegance – which exemplifies the countless qualities which make it irreplaceable in all of its fields. Whether as juice or grated peel, the lemon is utilized a thousand times a day – from the liquor industry to perfumes, from being used as an ingredient in foods to curing both minor and major ailments. The lemons smaller, delicate and more fragrant cousin, the lime, possesses all the same wonderful flavouring and healthful properties and I have grown to adore it as an ingredient as much as lemon, for all its subtly different qualities.

The Small Bites chapter includes tasty morsels, perfect to serve as appetizers, summer grazing plates or as part of a small plates style spread. In the Soups and Salads chapter, the addition of citrus brings bountiful life to simple salads, vigour to a cold soup, and of course rich complexity to Asian broths. Meat and Poultry is full of hearty meals with the zingy uplift of citrus. Fish and Seafood is one of the most classic pairings for citrus, with plenty of luxuriously simple dishes. Vegetable Sides provides some unique ways to make vegetables the star of the show. Finally, Sweets and Drinks includes everything from a lemon curd to a showstopping gin and tonic cake. I hope these tangy, fresh recipes add a bit of zest to your life.

SMALL BITES

MINI FETA AND LEMON SPANAKOPITA

I LOVE SERVING THESE NEAT LITTLE PARCELS TO FAMILY AND FRIENDS –
IT ALWAYS LOOKS LIKE YOU HAVE BEEN SLAVING AWAY, BUT REALLY NOTHING
COULD BE SIMPLER! I HAVE PLUMPED FOR THE TRADITIONAL GREEK FILLING OF
SALTY FETA CHEESE AND EARTHY SPINACH BENEATH CRISP BUTTERY PASTRY
– THE ADDITION OF LEMON ZEST BRINGS EVERYTHING TOGETHER BEAUTIFULLY.

1.5 kg/3¼ lb. spinach or chard, stems trimmed

1 tablespoon olive oil

2 medium onions, chopped

1 garlic clove, crushed

2 teaspoons finely ground nutmeg

a handful each of chopped fresh mint, dill and flat-leaf parsley leaves

200 g/7 oz. feta cheese, crumbled

4 spring onions/scallions, finely chopped

zest of 1 lemon

125 g/1⅛ sticks unsalted butter, melted

16 sheets of filo/Phyllo pastry

3–4 teaspoons white sesame seeds, to sprinkle

2 baking sheets, greased

MAKES 16 (TO SERVE 4)

Boil or steam the spinach or chard until just wilted. Drain, squeeze out the excess moisture and chop coarsely. Set aside in a large bowl.

Heat the olive oil in a small frying pan/skillet and cook the onions over a medium heat until golden. Stir in the garlic and nutmeg and fry for a few more minutes until fragrant. Remove from the heat and mix together with the spinach in the large bowl. Add all the herbs, feta cheese, spring onions/scallions and lemon zest and mix to evenly combine.

Preheat the oven to 180°C (350°F) Gas 4.

Have the prepared baking sheets, melted butter and filo/Phyllo pastry (covered in a damp kitchen cloth to prevent drying out) to hand. Lay a sheet of filo/Phyllo pastry out on the work surface and brush (but do not soak) all over with melted butter and fold lengthways into two thirds, brushing with more butter between each fold.

Put a rounded tablespoon of the spinach mixture at the bottom on one side of the narrow edge of the folded pastry sheet, leaving a border clear of filling. Fold one corner of the pastry diagonally over the filling to form a large triangle. Continue folding to the end of the pastry sheet, retaining the triangular shape. Repeat with the remaining ingredients to make 16 triangles in total, placing seam-side-down on the prepared baking sheets as you finish.

Brush the parcels with the remaining butter. Sprinkle with sesame seeds and bake in the preheated oven for 15 minutes until lightly browned. Transfer to a wire cooling rack and serve warm or cold.

SALMON AND KAFFIR LIME CAKES

AN INDISPENSABLE PART OF AUTHENTIC THAI COOKING, KAFFIR LIME
LEAVES ARE USED TO GIVE A SHARPLY AROMATIC EDGE TO MANY DISHES.
THESE FISHCAKES MAKE A WONDERFUL APPETIZER OR EVEN LIGHT LUNCH
SERVED WITH THE DIPPING SAUCE AND RICE AND SALAD ON THE SIDE.

500 g/1¼ lb. salmon fillets,
  skin removed

1 egg white

3 tablespoons fine rice flour

2 fresh kaffir lime leaves,
  shredded

1 tablespoon peeled and finely
  chopped fresh ginger

1 teaspoon wasabi paste

3 tablespoons chopped fresh
  flat-leaf parsley leaves

oil, for shallow frying

sliced green and red chillies/
  chiles, to garnish

LIME DIPPING SAUCE

juice of 2 limes

4 tablespoons soy sauce

2 tablespoons brown sugar

MAKES 20

Remove any bones from the salmon and finely dice into small cubes. In a
large bowl, combine the diced salmon with the egg white, rice flour, kaffir
lime leaves, ginger, wasabi and parsley. Mix together until well combined.

Preheat the oven to 120°C (250°F) Gas ½.

Pour in enough oil to coat the base of a frying pan/skillet and set over
a medium heat. Put 2 tablespoons of salmon mixture per cake into the
hot oil and cook for 35–45 seconds on each side until lightly golden.
Depending on the size of your pan, you can cook these in batches of
around six at a time. Drain on paper towels, then transfer to a non-stick
baking sheet and keep warm in the oven while you cook the rest.

To make the dipping sauce, simply mix
together the ingredients in a small dish.
Serve the warm fish cakes with the
dipping sauce and sprinkle with
sliced chillies/chiles to garnish.

MEXICAN CITRUS-MARINATED CEVICHE

THIS CLASSIC MEXICAN APPETIZER TRULY EMBRACES THE WONDERS OF CITRUS FLAVOURS. THE ACIDIC JUICES ESSENTIALLY 'COOK' THE FISH AND AT THE SAME TIME IMPART THEIR UNIQUE AND TASTY FLAVOUR. SO SIMPLE YET VERY IMPRESSIVE, THIS DISH CAN BE MADE UP TO TWO DAYS IN ADVANCE OF SERVING, AS LONG AS VERY FRESH FISH IS USED.

450 g/1 lb. mixed raw white fish fillets, such as hake, haddock and sole, skinned and pin boned (you can do this yourself with a pair of fish bone tweezers or ask your fishmonger)

juice of 3 unwaxed lemons

juice of 3 unwaxed limes

2 teaspoons chopped fresh oregano leaves

½ teaspoon cumin seeds

1 large ripe tomato, finely diced

1 small red onion, finely chopped

1 green chilli/chile, deseeded (optional) and finely chopped

a handful of fresh coriander/ cilantro leaves, chopped

a handful of fresh mint leaves, chopped

sea salt and freshly ground black pepper

2 tablespoons olive oil

SERVES 4

Cut all the fish fillets into 1 cm/⅓ in. cubes and place in a glass container or bowl with the lemon and lime juices and chopped oregano. Mix well, cover with clingfilm/plastic wrap and leave in the fridge for up to 12 hours. Any longer than this and the fish will become very mushy.

Meanwhile, toast the cumin seeds for a couple of minutes in a dry frying pan/skillet set over a medium heat, shaking the pan and stirring constantly until fragrant. Remove the seeds from the pan and let cool.

Drain and discard the citrus juices from the fish. Put the fish into a clean bowl and mix with the toasted cumin seeds, chopped tomato, onion, chilli/chile, coriander/cilantro and mint. Add salt and pepper to taste, drizzle over the oil and divide up into small bowls to serve. Alternatively, at this stage, the fish mixture will keep for up to two days in the refrigerator in an airtight container.

POTTED CRAB WITH BROWN SHRIMP BUTTER

A RATHER DECADENT, YET SIMPLE AND SATISFYING DISH TO SERVE AND EAT
AT SPECIAL OCCASIONS. PLEASE ENSURE ALL SEAFOOD IS AT ITS BEST.

150 g/1¼ sticks unsalted
butter

1 shallot, finely chopped

¼ teaspoon freshly grated
nutmeg

¼ teaspoon ground mace

¼ teaspoon sweet smoked
paprika

¼ teaspoon cayenne pepper

2 anchovy fillets, mashed

3 tablespoons dry sherry

400 g/14 oz. picked white
crab meat

100 g/3½ oz. picked brown
crab meat

zest and 3 teaspoons juice
of 2 lemons

50 g/2 oz. brown shrimps

sea salt and freshly ground
black pepper

day-old sourdough bread,
sliced and toasted, to serve

4–6 ramekin dishes

SERVES 4–6

Melt 100 g/1 stick minus 1 tablespoon of the butter in a saucepan, add
the shallot and cook until translucent. Stir in all the spices, anchovy fillets
and sherry. Cook over medium heat until the alcohol has evaporated.

Add both types of crab meat, the lemon zest and juice. Season to taste
with salt and pepper. Cook, stirring, for a couple of minutes and remove
from the heat as soon as the crab meat has warmed through. Divide
the mixture between the ramekins, filling just to the top and smoothing
the surfaces to level.

Melt the remaining butter, then mix in the brown shrimps and spoon
over the crab, dividing equally between the ramekins. Let cool and
then chill in the refrigerator for 2 hours until set. Serve with sliced
and toasted sourdough.

BEAN, LEMON AND HERB POTATO CAKES

THESE DELICIOUS POTATO CAKES ARE IDEAL FOR SUMMER ENTERTAINING..

350 g/12 oz. Jersey Royals or
Cornish New Potatoes, halved

150 g/1 cup fresh broad/fava
beans, shelled

zest of 2 lemons

2 tablespoons chopped fresh
mint

1 teaspoon ground coriander

150 g/¾ cup natural yogurt

oil, for shallow frying

SERVES 4

Cook the potatoes in boiling water for 10–15 minutes until tender, drain
and cool. Meanwhile cook the beans until just tender, drain and cool.
Place the beans in a food processor and blend to a coarse paste.

Crush the potatoes and stir in the bean paste, lemon zest, half the mint,
the coriander, 1 tablespoon of yogurt and some seasoning. Divide the
mixture into 4 and use your hands to shape into cakes.

Heat the oil in a large non-stick frying pan/skillet and fry the cakes for
3 minutes on each side until golden. Mix the remaining yogurt and mint
together and serve with potato cakes.

COURGETTE/ZUCCHINI FRITTERS

ZESTY, FRESH AND A GOOD WAY TO USE UP SURPLUS COURGETTES/ZUCCHINI.

750 g /1 lb. 10 oz. courgettes/
zucchinis, topped and tailed

sea salt and freshly ground
black pepper

freshly grated nutmeg

2 garlic cloves, finely chopped

2 generous handfuls of fresh
mint leaves, finely chopped

a handful of fresh chives,
chopped

1 tablespoon lemon thyme leaves

zest of 2 lemons

1 tablespoon rice flour or
cornflour/cornstarch

2 UK large/US extra-large eggs,
beaten

oil, for shallow frying

micro cress and lemon wedges,
to serve (optional)

MAKES 8

Coarsely grate the courgettes/zucchini, put them in a colander and
sprinkle with 1 teaspoon of salt. Leave for half an hour to degorge.

Using your hands, squeeze as much water as you can out of the courgettes/
zucchini. Place in a bowl and mix well with the remaining ingredients.

Preheat the oven to 120°C (250°F) Gas ½.

Heat the oil in a large non-stick frying pan/skillet over a moderate heat.
Place a tablespoon of batter into the pan and flatten to a 9-cm/3½-in.
round. Repeat for 3 more fritters and fry until golden and firm – try to
resist prodding and poking at them too much while they are cooking.
Flip and repeat until golden. They should take about 6 minutes in total
to cook. Drain on paper towels and keep warm in the oven while you fry
the rest of the batch.

Serve the fritters sprinkled with a garnish of micro cress and extra lemon
wedges to squeeze over, if you like.

THE HISTORY OF THE LEMON

THE LEMON, ONE OF THE BEST-KNOWN CITRUS FRUITS, IS A CULTURAL AND CULINARY PHENOMENON. MANY FRUITS ARE GROWN FAR FROM THEIR LANDS OF ORIGIN AND THIS IS CERTAINLY TRUE OF THE LEMON WHICH HAS BEEN GROWN ACROSS THE GLOBE FOR CENTURIES.

The lemon most likely originated from the citron, which has more varieties than any other citrus. Most sources suggest that lemons (or at least citrons) were originally found in Asia. Their travels, packed deep in merchants' saddle bags, owe much to economic history and echo the classic, ancient voyages of travel and discovery.

Citron seeds have been found in excavations dating back to 4000BC in regions of the ancient civilization of Mesopotamia (a vast area that covers modern-day Iraq and parts of Kuwait, Syria and Turkey). It is thought that they were first cultivated in Persia (now modern-day Iran) before being brought to Greece by military expedition and

introduced to Palestine by Greek colonists around 200BC. A Jewish coin minted in 136BC even shows the fruit on one side. In addition, citrus fruit is mentioned by early Christian writers.

Lemons grow wild in northern India, in the foothills of the Himalayas, and were introduced from there into Palestine and Egypt in the 10th century, and to Europe after the Indian conquests of Alexander the Great. Their spread beyond and throughout the Mediterranean region and Europe was a fringe benefit of the Jewish diaspora and the march of Roman legions. It was Spaniards who brought the citron to Puerto Rico in 1640 and then to Florida, where they were first commercially grown in 1880.

Arabs also contributed to the spread, introducing citrus fruits alongside their settlements and trade routes. Colonization and civilization have seen citrus successfully transported, planted and grown with staggering success and innumerable new varieties. Arabian knowledge of irrigation and agriculture is partly responsible for the historic hybridization and growth of citrus following the intense commercial traffic routes from Asia to Europe, known as The Silk Road and The Spice Route – important trade routes over land and sea.

Religion, too, has played its part alongside economic value, as citrus fruits hold deeply symbolic significance. For example, for Lubavitch Jews, the Diamante citron plays an essential role during Sukkot, the Feast of the Tabernacles.

Citrus fruits and lemons in particular, it seems, have a long-standing, powerful, peculiar and irresistible appeal. Loved for their unparalleled taste, vibrancy, versatility and deep fragrance in flowers, leaves, fruit and wood, their widespread uses – both practical and edible – only add to their allure. Lemon trees are faster growing then orange trees, and have fruit that writer Helena Attlee describes as 'eternal, neither rotting nor falling from the tree'. In addition, lemon trees are usually more productive

than other citrus varieties and will withstand more neglect and grow in a greater variety of soils. They are recognized as hardy and easily developed, grafted and cultivated with low-maintenance crops. They have the ability to travel well, their fruit protected by pith and peel.

It is no coincidence that these virtues have led to so many successful varieties and to such global spread. There is probably no other fruit tree that will adapt with such ease. Whatever the exact origins and history, it is undeniable that for thousands of years people have felt compelled to cultivate, share, harvest, paint and imbue symbolic significance on citrus and that it has an important role in ancient colonization and civilization.

DEEP-FRIED BABY LEMON CALAMARI

THIS SIMPLEST OF DISHES, PREPARED WELL, FILLS ME WITH NOSTALGIA FOR MY BEACH HOLIDAYS AS A CHILD IN PUGLIA; AFTER A DAY IN THE SUN IT WOULD MORE THAN SATISFY THE NEED FOR SOMETHING SALTY AND CRISP. I ENJOY THIS LEMON CALAMARI NOW AS AN ADULT WITH A GLASS OF CHILLED WHITE WINE.

500 g/1¼ lb. baby calamari, cleaned

50 g/generous ⅓ cup 'oo' Italian flour or plain/ all-purpose flour (rice flour also works)

1 teaspoon freshly ground cumin seeds

very finely grated zest of 1 lemon

groundnut/peanut oil, for deep-frying

2 teaspoons dried oregano

salt and freshly ground black pepper

2 quartered lemons, to serve

sliced red and green chillies/ chiles, to serve (optional)

chopped fresh coriander/ cilantro, to serve (optional)

SERVES 4

Slice the calamari into thin rings. In a large bowl, mix together the flour, ground cumin seeds, lemon zest, and a little salt and pepper.

Heat the oil to 180°C (350°F) in a medium non-stick saucepan.

Toss the calamari in the flour mixture and cumin, and shake away any excess. Deep-fry in batches for around 4 minutes until lightly browned and tender. Remove with a slotted spoon and drain the excess oil on paper towels.

Sprinkle the calamari with the oregano. Add a squeeze of lemon juice and a sprinkle of chilli/chile, if desired, and serve.

CABBAGE LEAVES STUFFED WITH GOCHUJANG AND LIME PORK

GOCHUJANG IS A FIERY KOREAN CHILLI PASTE, WHICH PARTNERS SO WELL WITH THE FRAGRANT SWEETNESS OF LIME. IT IS EASY TO FIND, EITHER IN GROCERY STORES OR ONLINE. THESE DELICIOUS APPETIZERS ARE COLOURFUL, SIMPLE AND PACKED FULL OF FLAVOUR.

12 large Chinese cabbage or Savoy cabbage leaves

400 g/15 oz. minced/ground pork

2 tablespoons gochujang paste

zest of 3 limes

4 spring onions/scallions, finely sliced

75 g/3 oz. fresh ginger, peeled and finely grated

2 garlic cloves, finely chopped

4 teaspoons tamari soy sauce

1 tablespoon toasted sesame oil

1 tablespoon Chinese rice vinegar

CUCUMBER RELISH

1 medium cucumber

2 teaspoons clear honey

1 garlic clove, finely chopped

1 teaspoon tamari soy sauce

1 teaspoon toasted sesame oil

juice of 1 lime

2 medium fresh red chillies/chiles, finely chopped

sea salt and freshly ground black pepper

lime wedges, to serve

SERVES 4

Cut the tough ribs out of the leaves. Finely chop the ribs, place in a large bowl and set aside.

Submerge the whole leaves in boiling water for 3 minutes. Refresh in a bowl of ice cold water, drain and pat dry with paper towel. Set aside.

Mix the minced/ground pork with the chopped cabbage leaves, gochujang paste, lime zest, spring onions/scallions, ginger, garlic, tamari soy sauce, toasted sesame oil and Chinese rice vinegar. Season with salt and pepper.

Divide the pork mixture between the leaves. Fold in the top and bottom and then lightly roll up to encase the filling. Place seam-side-down on a baking sheet as you finish each one. Steam in batches in a steamer or metal sieve/strainer set over a pan of boiling water for 15 minutes until the pork inside is cooked through.

To make the cucumber relish, bash the cucumber with a rolling pin, then roughly chop and place in a bowl. Add the honey, garlic, tamari soy sauce, sesame oil, lime juice and chopped chillies/chiles and toss everything together. Season to taste with salt and black pepper.

Serve the parcels warm with the relish on the side for dipping and extra lime wedges to squeeze over.

LEMON AND MOZZARELLA FOCACCIA BITES

FOCACCIA GETS ITS NAME FROM THE LATIN WORD FOR 'HEARTH'. THIS RECIPE HAS TAKEN ME YEARS TO PERFECT – EXPERIENCE AND PRACTICE HAVE HELPED.

YEAST STARTER OR BIGA

100 g/3½ oz. strong white/ bread flour

2.5 g/1½ oz. fresh yeast, crumbled

DOUGH

250 g/1¾ cups strong white/ bread flour, plus extra for dusting

2 teaspoons fine sea salt

2 teaspoons fresh yeast, crumbled or 2 teaspoons instant dried yeast

approx. 200 ml/scant 1 cup warm water

1 tablespoon olive oil, plus extra for oiling the bowl

3 tablespoons biga

TO FINISH

coarse sea salt

freshly ground black pepper

leaves from 2–3 fresh rosemary sprigs

125 g/4½ oz. buffalo mozzarella cheese, grated

zest of 1 unwaxed lemon

good-quality extra virgin olive oil, to drizzle

lemon dipping oil, to serve (optional)

a baking sheet, oiled

SERVES 6

To make the biga, sift the flour into a large bowl and make a well in the centre. Crumble the fresh yeast into 150 ml/5 oz. body temperature water and add the mixture to the well. Mix together to form a batter. Cover with a damp cloth and leave at room temperature. Keep dampening the cloth for 24–36 hours, but no longer.

For the dough, mix together the flour and salt in a large bowl and run your hands through the flour to warm it a little. Make a well in the centre.

In a separate bowl, dissolve the crumbled fresh yeast in 2 tablespoons of the warm water and pour this into the well along with 1 tablespoon of olive oil and the biga. Alternatively, add the instant dried yeast. Use a wooden spoon to stir while adding the remaining warm water slowly, mixing until you get a raggy dough that is neither too wet nor too dry.

Turn the dough out onto a lightly floured surface and knead firmly for 10 minutes. Test to see if it is ready – if you can stretch it easily without it breaking then the gluten should have developed sufficiently. Return the dough to a clean, oiled bowl and rub a little oil on top of it. Cover with a damp kitchen cloth and leave in a warm place for 1½ hours to rise.

Uncover the dough, knock it back, and knead for another 5 minutes. Cover with the damp cloth in the bowl again and rest for 10 minutes.

Roll the dough out into a round, approx. 28 cm/11 in. in diameter and at least 1 cm/⅓-in. thick. Place on the oiled baking sheet, cover with the damp cloth, and leave to rise for 30 minutes.

Preheat the oven to 200°C (400°F) Gas 6.

Using your fingertips, make dimples in the dough, then sprinkle with the coarse sea salt, black pepper and rosemary. Leave to rest for 10 minutes.

Bake the dough in the middle of the preheated oven for 30 minutes, until golden brown. Remove from the oven and transfer to a wire rack. Sprinkle with the mozzarella and lemon zest while still hot, allowing the cheese to melt onto the surface. When cool, drizzle the bread with extra virgin olive oil, then cut into wedges and enjoy with the lemon dipping oil, if liked.

DEEP-FRIED BABY ARTICHOKES WITH LEMON, MINT AND ANCHOVY DRESSING

I GROW ARTICHOKES IN MY GARDEN AND EAGERLY AWAIT THEM COMING INTO SEASON. THIS IS THE PERFECT RECIPE FOR YOUNG ARTICHOKES, WHICH HAVE NO FIDDLY 'CHOKE' TO REMOVE. EVEN THOUGH MY HUSBAND THINKS ANCHOVIES ARE EVIL, HE LIKES THIS DRESSING, IT ADDS A DELICIOUS PIQUANCY TO THE DISH.

BATTER

375 g/2¾ cups plus 1½ tablespoons '00' Italian flour or plain/all-purpose flour

a pinch of sea salt

125 ml/generous ½ cup olive oil

80 ml/generous ⅓ cup sparkling water

1 UK large/US extra-large egg white

ANCHOVY DRESSING

6 anchovy fillets in olive oil

a generous handful of fresh mint, leaves only

1 tablespoon lemon juice

1 tablespoon red wine vinegar

120 ml/½ cup fruity extra virgin olive oil

ARTICHOKES

12 small young artichokes

2 tablespoons lemon juice, for acidulating the water

2 lemons

groundnut/peanut oil, for deep-frying

a deep-fat fryer or large pan suitable for deep-frying

SERVES 4–6

Start by making the batter – there will be more than you need but it keeps well in the fridge. Sift the flour into a large bowl, add a pinch of salt and make a well in the centre. Pour in the olive oil, whisking until combined. Add the sparkling water and whisk until combined. In a separate bowl, whisk the egg white to firm peaks and then gently fold this in. Set the batter aside in the fridge until needed.

To make the anchovy dressing, drain and rinse the anchovies and pat dry. Add these to a food processor along with the rest of the dressing ingredients and blend to make a lovely green paste. Taste and add more oil or lemon juice if liked.

To prepare the artichokes, use a sharp knife to trim and peel the stems and cut off the tops of the tough outer leaves at the point where their colour becomes dark. Cut the artichokes in half lengthwise and remove the hairy choke if needed (in young artichokes there will not be any choke). Immerse the vegetables in a bowl of water acidulated with a little lemon juice. Slice the whole lemons into fairly thin, even rounds – they will be deep-fried so don't make them so thin they will fall apart.

When ready to cook, drain the artichokes from their lemon water and pat dry with paper towels. Heat the groundnut/peanut oil in a deep-fat fryer or large pan to around 180°C (350°F). Dip each artichoke in the batter and turn to give an even coating, then lift out to let the excess batter drain away. Lower carefully into the hot oil and deep-fry the artichokes in batches of 4 –5 at a time until golden. Remove with a slotted spoon and drain on paper towels. Batter and deep-fry the lemon slices in the same way.

Serve the hot artichokes and lemon slices with the anchovy dressing on a warmed plate and enjoy.

SPINACH, PEA AND RICOTTA GNOCCHI

I HAVE SO MANY RECIPES FOR GNOCCHI, EACH ONE AS GOOD AS THE NEXT.
I LOVE THE COLOUR AND TEXTURE OF THIS PARTICULAR RECIPE WHICH IS MADE
WITH HOME-MADE LEMON RICOTTA AND FRESH PEAS. I FIRST ENJOYED EATING
THIS GNOCCHI IN VERONA WITH SOME FAMILY FRIENDS.

LEMON RICOTTA

1 litre/4 cups minus
   3 tablespoons whole milk

1 teaspoon salt

4 teaspoons lemon juice

GNOCCHI

225 g/4½ cups fresh spinach
   leaves

225 g/1½ cups shelled fresh
   peas

1 tablespoon torn fresh sage
   leaves, plus a handful of
   whole leaves to finish the
   dish

2 free-range eggs

220 g/1 cup lemon ricotta (see
   recipe above)

a pinch of freshly grated
   nutmeg

75 g/1 cup freshly grated
   Parmesan cheese

3 tablespoons breadcrumbs

5 tablespoons plain/
   all-purpose flour

150 g/ unsalted butter

salt and freshly ground black
   pepper

*a large square of muslin/
   cheesecloth and cook's
   string, for the ricotta*

SERVES 4

First, make the ricotta. Place the milk, salt and lemon juice in a saucepan. Bring to the boil, then simmer for 15 minutes, or until the curds float on the top. Transfer the curds to the muslin/cheesecloth using a slotted spoon. Tie up and hang over a kitchen sink to drain for 2–3 hours. Your lemon ricotta cheese should now be ready to use.

Wash the spinach leaves and remove the stems. Put in a large saucepan with only the water still clinging to the leaves after washing. Cover and cook for 2 minutes until wilted. Drain through a sieve/strainer and squeeze until dry. Cook the peas in a little water for about 8 minutes until just tender. Drain well. Put the spinach, torn sage leaves and peas in a food processor and chop finely.

Lightly beat the eggs and add to the spinach mixture with the lemon ricotta, nutmeg, salt, pepper, half the Parmesan cheese, breadcrumbs and nearly all the flour. Mix together well, adding more flour if necessary. (The mixture should be firm enough for a spoon to stand upright in it.)

Preheat the oven to 120°C (250°F) Gas ½.

Place a large serving dish in the oven to warm. Meanwhile, using well-floured hands take 3 heaped dessertspoonfuls of the gnocchi mixture and roll lightly into small ovals. Use the prongs of a fork to gently press down on each oval and make a small indent. Bring a large pan of water to the boil, then reduce the heat. Drop a few gnocchi at a time into the water and cook for 4–5 minutes or until they rise to the surface. Using a slotted spoon, remove from the pan and drain. Keep warm in the serving dish in the low oven while you cook the rest.

To finish the dish, melt the butter in a saucepan with the whole sage leaves and pour over the gnocchi. Serve sprinkled with the remaining Parmesan cheese.

SOUPS AND SALADS

SMOKED TROUT, CUCUMBER AND COCONUT SALAD WITH DOSAI

THERE ARE MANY VARIETIES OF DOSA, AND MOST REQUIRE THE BATTER TO FERMENT OVERNIGHT. I'VE ADAPTED A GODHUMA DOSA RECIPE BECAUSE THESE REQUIRE NO FERMENTATION, MAKING THEM IDEAL FOR SPEEDY DINNERS. FOR A SUPER-FAST MEAL, YOU COULD BUY READY-MADE DOSAI.

400g/14 oz. smoked trout, coarsely flaked, bones removed

2 Lebanese or 1 English cucumber, sliced

2 handfuls of fresh coriander/cilantro

25 g/scant ½ cup shredded coconut

½ red onion, thinly sliced

2 fresh kaffir lime leaves, thinly sliced, plus extra to serve

juice of 1 ½ limes

1 tablespoon vegetable oil

Cos lettuce leaves, to serve (optional)

GREEN CHILLI DOSAI

150 g/1¼ cups wholemeal flour

50 g/½ cup rice flour

15 g /½ oz. (2.5-cm/ 1-in. piece) ginger, finely grated

1 long green chilli/chile, finely chopped

1 teaspoon cumin seeds

salt and freshly ground black pepper

SERVES 4

Prepare the batter for the dosai. Combine the flours, ginger, chilli/chile and cumin seeds in a large bowl, then whisk in 430 ml/15 oz. cold water, season to taste, whisk to combine and set aside.

Combine the trout, cucumbers, coriander/cilantro, coconut, onion, kaffir lime leaves and lime juice in a large bowl and set aside.

Heat ½ teaspoon of the oil in a large frying pan/ skillet over high heat. Add 2 tablespoons of the dosa batter, swirl to thinly coat the base of the pan, cook until golden (1 minute), then flip and cook until crisp (1 minute). Transfer to a serving plate and cover with foil to keep warm and repeat with the remaining oil and batter. Stack the cooked dosai between sheets of baking parchment to prevent them sticking to each other.

Serve with the smoked trout salad, extra kaffir lime leaves and lettuce leaves, if using.

WARM CHICKEN AND LEMON COUSCOUS SALAD

THIS DISH IS A FAMILY FAVOURITE, AND IT'S SO QUICK TO MAKE AT THE END OF A BUSY DAY, ESPECIALLY AS MANY OF THE INGREDIENTS WILL ALREADY BE IN YOUR STORECUPBOARD. IT IS ALSO GOOD FOR SUMMER ENTERTAINING

4 chicken breast fillets

1 tablespoon olive oil

freshly ground black pepper

2 lemons, halved

LEMON COUSCOUS

170 g/1 cup couscous

300 ml/1¼ cups boiling chicken stock or water

2 tablespoons butter

2 tablespoons shredded lemon rind

2 tablespoons salted capers, rinsed

3 tablespoons shredded fresh sage leaves

20 g/¼ cup slivered almonds

SERVES 4

Preheat a grill pan/griddle or a barbecue. Brush the chicken with the olive oil and sprinkle with pepper. Cook the chicken in the hot grill pan/griddle or on the barbecue for 5 minutes each side or until cooked through and the juices run clear. Set aside and cover to keep warm. Place the lemons on the grill or barbecue, cut-side down, and cook for 1 minute.

To make the lemon couscous, place the couscous in a bowl and pour over the chicken stock or water. Cover lightly with a lid or clingfilm/plastic wrap and stand for 5 minutes or until the liquid has been absorbed.

Heat the butter in a large frying pan/skillet over medium heat. Add the lemon rind, capers, sage and almonds and cook for 7 minutes or until the almonds are lightly toasted. Add the couscous to the pan and toss to combine.

To serve, pile the lemon couscous onto serving plates and top with the sliced grilled chicken and grilled lemons. Serve with salad leaves.

BANG BANG CHICKEN SALAD

COLOURFUL, CRUNCHY AND SO SIMPLE TO PREPARE, THIS CERTAIN CROWD PLEASER CAN BE PREPARED AHEAD OF TIME. THE LIME IN THIS DISH SHOWS ITS TRUE COLOURS FOR BEING ABLE TO SO CLEVERLY INTERTWINE ALL THE FLAVOURS TOGETHER TO CREATE A CRISP, FRAGRANT DISH.

200 g/7 oz. dried rice noodles

125 g/2 cups beansprouts

1 medium organic carrot, sliced into 5-cm/2-in. strips

3 spring onions/scallions, finely shredded lengthways

½ cucumber cut into 5-cm/ 2-in. batons

2 medium red chillies/chiles, deseeded and finely sliced

2 large cooked, skinless chicken breasts (see note)

1 tablespoon sesame seeds

60 g/½ cup roasted peanuts, roughly chopped

a small handful of fresh coriander/cilantro leaves

DRESSING

2 tablespoons groundnut oil

2 tablespoons toasted sesame oil

zest and juice from 2 unwaxed limes

8 cm/3-in. piece of fresh ginger, grated

2 tablespoons tamari soy sauce

a pinch of chilli flakes (optional)

SERVES 4

Place the noodles in a shallow dish. Pour over boiling water to cover and leave for 12 minutes until softened, stirring occasionally. Drain in a colander.

Meanwhile, cook the beansprouts in boiling water for 2–3 minutes, drain well, then refresh under ice cold water. Drain in a colander.

On a large plate arrange the carrot, spring onions/scallions, cucumber, beansprouts and chillies/chiles. Shred the chicken and arrange with the noodles on top of the vegetables.

To make the dressing, place the oils in a food processor with the lime zest and juice, ginger, tamari and chilli flakes, if using. Whizz to a smooth dressing.

Spoon the dressing over the top of the salad and sprinkle with sesame seeds, chopped peanuts and fresh coriander/cilantro to serve.

Note: To poach chicken breasts, roughly chop a carrot, onion and stick of celery. Place in a pan with cold water over low heat. Bring to a gentle boil, add the chicken breasts, cover with a lid and cook for 20 minutes, or until the juices run clear.

LEMON SUMMER GRAIN SALAD

I RECOMMEND USING POUCHES OF READY-COOKED GRAINS AS THEY ARE SO
CONVENIENT (YOU COULD COOK YOUR OWN SELECTION OF GRAINS IF YOU
WISH, BUT THIS MAKES THE PREPARATION MORE TIME-CONSUMING).

2 courgettes/zucchini, thinly
sliced lengthways

mild olive oil, for brushing

1 tablespoon zatar

155 g/1 cup fresh peas

2 x 250 g/8 oz. pouches of
ready-cooked grains (such
as a mixture of barley,
wheatberries, spelt and rice)

a handful of fresh mint leaves

75 g/3 handfuls of pea shoots

DRESSING

zest and juice of 2 lemons

1 tablespoon harissa

3 tablespoons olive oil

SERVES 4

Heat a griddle or barbecue to hot. Brush the courgettes/zucchini with oil,
sprinkle over the zatar and cook in batches for 2 minutes on each side
until tender and seared. Remove from the heat and set aside. Tip the peas
into a pan of boiling water, cook for 3 minutes, then drain and set aside.

Tip the pouches of grains into a large bowl and break up with a fork.

For the dressing, whisk together the lemon zest and juice, harissa and
olive oil. Add to the grains and toss to coat evenly.

Gently combine the courgettes/zucchini, peas, mint leaves and pea
shoots with the dressed grains. Serve immediately.

GRILLED LETTUCE AND SPELT LEMON SALAD

I ADORE ALL LETTUCE LEAVES. I FIND EATING LEAVES IMMENSELY
PLEASURABLE AFTER A MEAL AND VERY REFRESHING AFTER A FISH DISH.
THIS SALAD IS A STAND-ALONE SALAD BUT COULD BE SERVED WITH A STEAK.
I LOVE ALL THE CRUNCH AND TASTY FLAVOURS THAT COMBINE SO WELL.

75 g/½ cup spelt (grains)

2 slices sourdough bread

3 tablespoons olive oil

2 Little Gem or Romaine
  lettuces, quartered

a generous handful of tarragon
  leaves

a handful of fresh flat-leaf
  parsley, roughly chopped

50 g/⅔ cup Parmigiano
  Reggiano, shaved

DRESSING

grated zest and segments
  of 1 unwaxed lemon

1 teaspoon clear honey

2 teaspoons pernod

1 small preserved lemon,
  halved, deseeded and
  thinly sliced

1 garlic clove, crushed

1 small shallot, finely chopped

2 tablespoons olive oil

sea salt and freshly ground
  black pepper

SERVES 4

Preheat the oven to 220°C (425°F) Gas Mark 7.

Bring a small pan of water to the boil, add the spelt and cook according
to the pack instructions. Drain, refresh and set aside.

For the dressing, add the lemon zest and segments to a bowl along with
the honey, pernod, preserved lemon, garlic, shallot and 2 tablespoons
of the olive oil, plus a little salt and black pepper. Mix well.

Drizzle the bread with 2 tablespoons of olive oil, place on a baking sheet
and bake for 6–8 minutes until golden. Turn the bread over and bake for
a further 3–4 minutes.

Heat the griddle pan, brush the lettuce quarters with the remaining oil
and griddle until lightly coloured on the outside.

Place the lettuce quarters on a serving platter. Tear the toasted bread
into small pieces and scatter over the lettuce quarters along with the
spelt and the lemon dressing. Garnish with the tarragon, parsley and
Parmegiano shavings and serve.

PEKING DUCK SALAD

I LOVE THE DARK RICH COLOUR OF THE DUCK IN CONTRAST TO THE VARYING SHADES OF GREEN FROM THE VEGETABLES. THIS IS A QUICK, IMPRESSIVE AND VERY SATISFYING DISH, PERFECT WHEN TIME IS SHORT AND YOU HAVE HUNGRY MOUTHS TO FEED.

2 duck breast fillets, skin on, (approx. 160 g/5½ oz. each)

2 tablespoons hoisin sauce

1 tablespoon groundnut/ peanut oil

2 tablespoons lime juice

1 small cucumber, thinly sliced, lengthways, into ribbons

100 g/2½ small bunches bok choy/pak choi, chopped

4 spring onions/scallions, finely sliced

salt and freshly ground black pepper

SERVES 4

Brush the duck all over with half of the hoisin sauce.

Heat the groundnut/peanut oil in a frying pan/skillet. Add the duck, skin side down, and cook for 5 minutes or until the skin is crisp. Turn the duck and cook for a further 5 minutes or until cooked as desired. Reserve the meat juices, to serve. Cover the duck, stand for 5 minutes and then slice thinly.

Whisk the lime juice and the meat juices in a large bowl. Add the duck, cucumber, bok choy/pak choi and spring onions/scallions and mix. Season to taste and serve.

WARM LENTIL SALAD WITH MARINATED COW'S MILK FETA

THIS SALAD IS ABSOLUTELY DIVINE STUFFED INTO WARM PITA BREADS.
I HAD AN AVERSION TO LENTILS BASED ON A PREJUDICE FROM THE 1970S,
BUT GREEN PUY LENTILS WON ME OVER.

210 g/4 cups puy lentils

1 small red (bell) pepper

1 small yellow (bell) pepper

2 tablespoons olive oil

2 garlic cloves, crushed

3-cm/1-in. piece of fresh ginger, peeled and very finely chopped

1 teaspoon ground cumin

$\frac{1}{2}$–$\frac{3}{4}$ teaspoon ground coriander

2 tablespoons pinenuts, lightly toasted in a dry pan

10 cherry tomatoes, halved

275 g/2 cups marinated cow's milk feta, cubed

sea salt and freshly ground black pepper

SALAD DRESSING

75 ml/$\frac{1}{2}$ cup olive oil

2 tablespoons red wine vinegar

6 g/$\frac{1}{4}$ cup roughly chopped fresh mint

zest from 3 unwaxed lemons, juice from 2 lemons

SERVES 6-8

Preheat the oven to 200°C (400°F) Gas 6.

Place the lentils in a medium saucepan and cover with cold water. Bring to the boil. Turn down heat and simmer until tender (about 25 minutes). Drain well.

Cut the peppers into 1-cm/$\frac{1}{2}$-in. strips and toss in 1 tablespoon of the olive oil seasoned with salt and pepper. Place the peppers on a baking sheet and roast for 7–10 minutes until tender.

Heat the remaining oil in a small frying pan/skillet. Add the garlic and ginger and sauté gently for 1 minute. Remove the pan from heat, add the cumin and coriander and stir well. Set aside.

To make the dressing, combine the oil, vinegar, mint, lemon zest and juice in a serving bowl.

Add the lentils, peppers, half the pinenuts, cherry tomatoes, half the feta and seasoning to the serving bowl and combine.

Scatter over the remaining pinenuts and feta and serve.

SEARED BEEF SALAD

THIS DISH HAS A HINT OF AN ORIENTAL FEEL BUT THE INGREDIENTS ARE MAINLY FROM THE BRITISH ISLES. I RECOMMEND USING THE VERY BEST STEAKS THAT YOU CAN FIND.

4 medium beetroot/beets

400 g/14 oz. sirloin steak

2 tablespoons olive oil

1 tablespoon horseradish sauce

grated zest and juice from 2 lemons

2 spring onions/scallions, trimmed and sliced

4 medium organic carrots, peeled and roughly grated

1 tablespoon good-quality balsamic vinegar

sea salt and freshly ground black pepper

SERVES 4

Place the beetroot/beets in a large pan of water, bring to the boil, reduce the heat and simmer for 30 minutes. Drain the beetroot/beets and set aside to cool. Once cool, carefully peel off the skin and grate.

Season the sirloin steak with salt and pepper and brush with olive oil. Heat a griddle to hot and sauté the steak, 3–4 minutes on each side for rare, 8–10 minutes for medium, turning once.

In a large bowl combine the beetroot/beets, horseradish, lemon zest and juice, spring onions/scallions, carrots and balsamic vinegar. Slice the beef and serve with the salad.

THE HISTORY OF THE LIME

THE LIME IS A YELLOW CITRUS FRUIT RESEMBLING A SMALL LEMON.
IT IS THE MOST TENDER OF ALL THE CITRUS FRUITS WITH A THIN SKIN,
AND ITS PULP IS PALE AND FILLED WITH A VERY SHARP ACID JUICE.

The lime is classed as a shrub but when given room to grow, it forms a small tree. Its exact origin is unknown, but it is presumed to be a hybrid of domesticated citrons and a wild species of Papeda, a non-commercial citrus subgenus. Limes generally grow only in climates where the temperature does not fall much below 20–28°C (68–82°F), thus limiting commercial production to temperate zones. Limes are grown extensively in Mexico, South Florida, the Caribbean and South-East Asia.

True limes are of two types. Persian limes, including the seedless Bearss variety, also known as Tahitian limes, are the most common in northern US markets because they are fairly hardy and easier to cultivate, transport and store thanks to their thicker skins. They have a sweeter taste than Key Limes, the other true lime, because they possess a greater sugar and citric acid content. The fruit is dark green when young and light yellow at full ripeness, and the pulp is juicy and seedless.

Mexican limes, or Key limes, are the standard bartenders' limes and are the only truly tropical species of citrus. They are small, round and pale in colour. Unlike Persian limes, they are more yellow than green when ripe. They also tend to be smaller, more aromatic, more acidic and, therefore, more sour than the popular Persian lime.

Ancient folklore among the Sinhala people of the island of Sri Lanka tells how limes originated during a fight between two cobra gods. Their fangs became the lime seeds and their poison became the acidic juice. Recent studies suggest an evolution that places the origin of true limes at Malaysia, about 2400km (1,500 miles) east of Sri Lanka.

Citrus cultivation radiated out from India along with civilization, but similar names for different citrus make the lime impossible to track separately. Writing in the 4th century BC, Antiphanes said citrus reached Greece from Persia. Ancient Rome had limes, lemons and citron, but not oranges. A Chinese agricultural treatise from 1178AD listed 27 citrus, including limes. Around the beginning of the 14th century, Italian medical writer Mattheus Silvaticus listed citron, oranges, lemons and limes as the known citrus. Meanwhile, limes were brought to the western Mediterranean countries by returning Crusaders in the 12th and 13th centuries.

It is thought that Columbus took citrus-fruit seed, probably including limes, to the West Indies on his second voyage in 1493. Portuguese traders probably carried it to Brazil, and it apparently arrived in Australia from Brazil around 1824. Limes reached California by way of Tahiti between 1850 and 1880 and arrived in Florida by 1883. From then on, the trees soon became widely distributed in the West Indies, Mexico and Florida. Lime growing reached south Florida from the Caribbean during the 1830s, with limited commercial production by 1880. Early groves in the Keys were planted in natural potholes filled with composted soil. Later groves were planted in rows of potholes blasted into limestone bedrock, and cultivation expanded after a 1906 hurricane destroyed a small pineapple industry. After the First World War, the Tahitian lime became a well-established commercial crop. Although it's hard to believe today, there was market resistance at first, buyers viewing it as a 'green lemon' but by the 1950s Key limes were widely distributed. However, growers reduced lime acreage just after 2000 due to citrus canker infection and falling wholesale prices.

While the Key lime was the first lime enjoyed by Europeans, the Persian lime soon took over in popularity because of its sweeter taste and relative hardiness compared to the more sensitive Key limes, which also have very thorny branches making them harder to pick.

AUGUST 1944 · TWENTY-FIVE CENTS

TOM YAM GOONG

THIS IS A THAI CLASSIC AND I HAVE ENJOYED EXPERIMENTING WITH
THIS DISH. IT IS VERY SIMPLE AND SUBTLE, WITH AN AMZING COLOUR.

12 large prawns/shrimp,
  shells on

1 tablespoon groundnut/
  peanut oil

4 shallots, finely chopped

a handful of fresh coriander/
  cilantro, roughly chopped,
  plus extra to serve

2 teaspoons chilli/chile paste

1½ litres/6¼ cups good-
  quality chicken stock

4 tender stalks of lemongrass,
  cut into 5-cm/2-in. pieces

4 fresh kaffir lime leaves

4 spring onions/scallions, cut
  into 3-cm/1-in. lengths

150 g/2¼ cups button
  mushrooms, sliced

3 plum tomatoes, peeled,
  deseeded and diced

2 fresh chillies/chiles,
  deseeded and finely sliced

2 tablespoons Thai fish sauce,
  plus extra to taste

100 ml/scant ½ cup fresh lime
  juice, plus extra to taste

SERVES 4

Prepare the prawns/shrimp by removing the heads and shells and
trimming out the dark waste line. Reserve the heads and shells. Butterfly
the prawns/shrimp and set aside.

Heat the oil in a large pan and sear the prawn/shrimp heads and shells
with the shallots and coriander/cilantro until the shells turn red. Add the
chilli/chile paste and stock and simmer for about 10 minutes. Strain the
heads and shells, reserving the stock, and rinse out the pan.

Return the reserved stock to the rinsed pan. Place the pan over the heat,
add the lemongrass, lime leaves, spring onions/scallions, mushrooms,
tomatoes, chillies/chiles and fish sauce and simmer for 5 minutes. Next,
add the prawns/shrimp to the pan. Add the lime juice and simmer for
a further 2–3 minutes until the prawns/shrimp turn pink. Adjust the
seasoning, adding more lime juice or fish sauce to taste.

Ladle the soup into warmed bowls and sprinkle with the reserved
coriander/cilantro, to serve.

PHO
VIETNAMESE NOODLE SOUP

PHO, PRONOUNCED 'FUH', IS A STAPLE ALL OVER VIETNAM. IT IS THOUGHT TO BE AN ADAPTATION OF THE CLASSIC FRENCH BEEF CASSEROLE POT-AU-FEU, DATING FROM THE TIME WHEN THE COUNTRY WAS PART OF FRENCH INDOCHINA. THERE ARE SO MANY VARIATIONS, I DO HOPE YOU WILL ENJOY MINE.

1 onion, halved

4 cm/1 $\frac{1}{2}$ -in. piece of fresh ginger, cut in half, peel on

1 kg/2$\frac{1}{4}$ lb. beef short ribs

1 bone marrow (approx. 200 g/7 oz.)

1 cinnamon stick

2 star anise

$\frac{1}{2}$ teaspoon fennel seeds

1 teaspoon coriander seeds

5 cloves

5 cardamom pods, crushed

2 tablespoons Thai fish sauce

2 teaspoons palm sugar

2 teaspoons salt

150 g/2 cups rice noodles

1 tablespoon groundnut/peanut oil

150 g/5 oz. skirt steak

3 spring onions/scallions, finely sliced diagonally

a handful each of fresh Thai basil leaves, mint leaves and coriander/cilantro leaves

juice of 2 limes

1 Thai chilli/chile, finely sliced

1 lime, cut into wedges

SERVES 4

Preheat the oven to 200°C (400°F) Gas 6.

Place the onion and ginger on a baking sheet lined with parchment paper and bake for 30 minutes until coloured.

Place the short ribs and marrow in a large, heavy saucepan and cover with cold water. Bring to the boil and remove any scum. Reduce the heat and simmer for 20 minutes. Drain the beef and bone marrow and rinse with cold water. Clean the pan.

Toast the spices in a dry frying pan/skillet until scented, then pound with a pestle and mortar.

Place the ribs and marrow along with the onion, ginger, spices, fish sauce, palm sugar and salt in a large pan. Pour enough cold water over to cover. Bring to the boil. Reduce the heat and simmer, uncovered, for 4 hours.

Strain the broth into a clean pan. Retain the meat from the ribs and marrow and discard the bones and aromatics. Top up the broth with cold water so you have 1 litre/4 cups.

Soak the rice noodles in cold water for 10 minutes.

Heat the oil in a frying pan/skillet and fry the steak for 4 minutes on each side. Slice while still warm.

Warm the broth and if necessary add more fish sauce, palm sugar and salt to taste. Drain the noodles and add to the broth, then add the meat from the ribs and marrow, the sliced steak and all the remaining ingredients except the lime wedges to the broth. Serve with lime wedges to the side.

AVGOLEMONO

AVGOLEMONO IS A CLASSIC GREEK SOUP FLAVOURED WITH EGGS AND LEMON. WHEN THE EGG AND LEMON JUICE MIXTURE IS ADDED, THE SOUP THICKENS TO A RICH CREAMY TEXTURE. PLEASE USE GOOD-QUALITY STOCK TO AVOID SPOILING THE DELICATE FLAVOUR, AND SEASON WITH CARE.

I litre/4 cups fresh chicken or vegetable stock

2 garlic cloves

115 g/½ cup long grain rice

3 eggs

juice of 2 unwaxed lemons

2 very thin lemon skins, halved, to garnish

a handful of flat-leaf parsley, chopped (optional)

salt and freshly ground black pepper

SERVES 4-6

Pour the stock into a large pan and bring to the boil. Add the garlic cloves and the rice and simmer for 15 minutes until the rice is tender. Remove and discard the garlic.

Beat the eggs lightly in a bowl. Beat in some of the lemon juice until the mixture is pale and foaming. Stir a ladleful of the hot stock into the egg mixture, beating continuously. Return the mixture to the stock, again stirring constantly. Almost immediately remove the stock from the heat. The soup must not boil or the eggs will curdle.

Adjust the seasoning with salt and pepper and add just enough of the remaining lemon juice to give the soup a good, sharp taste. Garnish with the lemon and parsley, if desired, and serve.

CHILLED AVOCADO AND PEA SOUP

MAKE WHEN AVOCADOS ARE JUST RIPE. THIS IS THE ULTIMATE 5-MINUTE SOUP WHEN YOU ARE FEELING OVERHEATED AND IN A RUSH AND IS IDEAL AS A NUTRITIOUS LUNCH ON A HOT SUMMER'S DAY. AVOCADOS ARE RICH IN POTASSIUM WHICH HELPS TO LEVEL BLOOD PRESSURE.

2 ripe avocados, peeled and stoned

½ cucumber, peeled and roughly chopped

200 g/1¾ cups fresh or frozen peas

zest of 2 unwaxed lemons and juice of 1

a generous handful of fresh mint, plus extra to garnish

2 tablespoons avocado oil, plus extra to serve

1 tablespoon pumpkin seeds, to garnish

a generous pinch of sweet smoked paprika, to garnish

an ice cube, to serve

SERVES 4

Put all the ingredients except the garnishes into a food processor and blend until smooth. Add 400 ml/1 ¾ cups of cold water, season to taste and blend again until thick and creamy.

Serve with an ice cube, pumpkin seeds, mint leaves, paprika and a splash of avocado oil in each bowl.

MEXICAN LIME SOUP WITH TOASTED GARLIC AND CITRUS JUICES

I RECOMMEND SERVING THIS REFRESHING, TRADITIONAL MEXICAN SOUP AS PART A MEXICAN FEAST. CHICKEN MAY BE ADDED, IF DESIRED.

15 garlic cloves

3 medium onions, finely chopped

3 unwaxed limes, peeled, deseeded and diced

3 chillies/chiles, finely chopped

2 tablespoons olive oil

1 green (bell) pepper, chopped

4 ripe tomatoes, diced

a small handful of fresh oregano leaves

1 litre/4 cups fresh chicken stock

rind and juice from ½ grapefruit

rind and juice from ½ orange

a handful of fresh coriander/ cilantro leaves

sea salt and freshly ground black pepper

SERVES 4–6

Preheat the oven to 200°C (400°F) Gas 6. Place the whole garlic cloves on a baking sheet and toast in the oven for 15 minutes. Peel the garlic and set aside.

Combine 1 chopped onion with the diced lime flesh and chopped chillies/ chiles in a bowl and set aside.

Heat the oil in a frying pan/skillet and sauté the remaining onions with the green (bell) pepper until softened. Add the tomatoes, oregano, toasted peeled garlic and chicken stock, and season with salt and pepper. Bring to the boil, then reduce the heat and simmer for about 12 minutes.

Just before serving, add the grapefruit and orange rind and juice and the coriander/cilantro (keep back a few leaves to garnish). Place several tablespoons of the onion, chilli/chile and lime mixture into each bowl, then ladle in the hot soup. Garnish with coriander/cilantro and serve immediately.

PORK DUMPLINGS IN LIME LEAF BROTH

THIS LIGHT AND FRAGRANT DISH IS SURPRISINGLY QUICK AND SIMPLE TO MAKE. IT'S AN EXCELLENT RECIPE FOR ENTERTAINING.

1 tablespoon groundnut/ peanut oil

300 g/10 ½ oz. minced/ diced pork

5 tablespoons hoisin sauce

1 garlic clove, crushed

3 tablespoons fresh coriander/cilantro leaves, chopped

20 dumpling or wonton wrappers

LIME LEAF BROTH

1 litre/4 cups chicken stock

3 slices of fresh ginger, peeled and cut into matchsticks

5 fresh kaffir lime leaves, lightly crushed, plus extra, shredded, to serve

2 tablespoons tamari soy sauce

SERVES 4

Heat the oil in a frying pan/skillet, add the minced pork and fry for 8 minutes, stirring, until browned.

To make the pork dumplings, combine the pork, hoisin sauce, garlic and coriander/cilantro leaves. Place 1 tablespoon of the mixture in the centre of each wonton wrapper. Brush a little water around the edges of the wrappers and press the edges together to seal.

To make the lime leaf broth, place the chicken stock, ginger, lime leaves and soy sauce in a saucepan and simmer over medium-high heat for 3 minutes. Add the dumplings a few at a time and cook for 8 minutes or until cooked through. Place the dumplings in bowls and pour some of the broth over to serve. Serve topped with finely shredded lime leaves.

Note: You can make the dumplings ahead of time and refrigerate them, covered with a slightly damp cloth.

MEAT
AND
POULTRY

ROAST CHICKEN WITH BROAD BEANS AND LEMON

I ADORE BROAD/FAVA BEANS AND GROW THEM EACH YEAR WITH VARYING DEGREES OF SUCCESS. MY HUSBAND LOVES CHICKEN AND THIS IS A PERFECT RELAXED, EASY SUMMER SUNDAY ROAST. IT'S TASTY, COLOURFUL AND EARTHY. SERVED WITH LEMON AND PARSLEY MASH (SEE RECIPE ON PAGE 117). SIMPLY DIVINE.

375 g/2½ cups fresh shelled broad/fava beans

2 tablespoons olive oil

1.5 kg/3¼ lb. free range organic chicken pieces, bone in, skin on

3 onions, roughly chopped

a handful of fresh thyme

rind and juice of 2 unwaxed lemons

3 garlic cloves, thinly sliced

350 ml/1½ cups fresh chicken stock

a handful of fresh mint leaves

2 tablespoons capers, rinsed

sea salt and freshly ground black pepper

SERVES 4

Preheat the oven to 200°C (400°F) Gas 6.

Bring a pan of water to the boil. Add the broad/fava beans and boil for 2 minutes. Drain and refresh under cold running water. Peel away the skins and discard.

Heat the oil in a large flameproof casserole dish over a high heat. Cook the chicken pieces in two batches, for 4 minutes on each side until browned. Remove from the dish and set aside.

Add the onion, thyme and lemon rind to the casserole dish and cook for 2 minutes. Return the chicken and any juices to the dish with the garlic and stock. Bring to the boil, and add salt and pepper. Transfer to the oven and cook uncovered for 40 minutes.

Stir in the broad/fava beans, 2 tablespoons of lemon juice and top with mint and capers. Season with salt and pepper to taste and serve.

SPICED CHICKEN WITH CHICKPEAS, CARROTS AND PRESERVED LEMON

THIS COLOURFUL DISH TAKES ITS INSPIRATION FROM NORTH AFRICA, AND THE RICH, SPICY FLAVOURS ARE VERY SATISFYING ON A COLD DAY.

½ teaspoon each ground cumin, ground coriander, ground fennel and chilli/chile powder

rind of 1 and juice of 2 lemons

1 teaspoon sea salt, plus extra to season

70 ml/5 tablespoons olive oil

8 chicken thighs, skin slashed in several places

2 carrots, halved lengthways and thinly sliced

2 baby fennel bulbs, thickly sliced, fronds reserved

1 onion, thinly sliced

2 garlic cloves, thinly sliced

a pinch of saffron threads

200 g/8 oz. canned cherry tomatoes

500 ml/2 cups plus 2 tablespoons chicken stock

120 ml/½ cup dry white wine

400 g/14 oz. canned chickpeas/garbanzo beans, drained and rinsed

½ cup each coarsely chopped flat-leaf parsley and mint, plus extra to serve

2 preserved lemon quarters (see page 101), rinsed, flesh discarded, rind finely chopped

freshly ground black pepper

SERVES 4

Preheat the oven to 220°C (425°F) Gas 7.

Combine the spices, lemon rind and sea salt in a small bowl. Rub the mixture liberally over the chicken pieces.

Heat half the olive oil in a large flameproof casserole dish over a medium-high heat. Add the chicken skin-side down and turn occasionally until browned.

Transfer the chicken to the preheated oven and roast for about 15 minutes, until cooked through.

Meanwhile, heat the remaining oil in a large frying pan/skillet. Add the carrot, fennel, onion, garlic and saffron and stir occasionally until the onion begins to soften. Add the tomatoes, stock and wine, bring to a simmer and cook for about 12–15 minutes or until the carrot is tender and the liquid reduces by half. Add the drained chickpeas/garbanzo beans, herbs, lemon juice and preserved lemon rind, season to taste and serve hot with the spiced roast chicken, scattered with the fennel fronds and extra herbs.

SKEWERED LAMB WITH BOCCONCINI CENTRES AND ORZO SALAD

THE BETTER THE QUALITY THE LAMB, THE TASTIER THE DISH WILL BE. SERVE WITH ORZO SALAD, OR MINTED BOILED POTATOES.

450 g/1 lb. minced/ground lamb

80 g/1½ cups sun-dried tomatoes in oil, drained and finely chopped

3 garlic cloves, finely chopped

¾ of a preserved lemon, rind, finely chopped

1 tablespoon olive oil, plus extra for shallow frying

3 tablespoons finely chopped fresh flat-leaf parsley

1½ teaspoons finely chopped fresh oregano leaves

75 g/3 oz. bocconcini balls

24 cherry tomatoes

24 basil leaves

sea salt and freshly ground black pepper

ORZO PASTA SALAD

150 g/1½ cups orzo pasta

a generous handful of fresh mint, coarsely chopped

1 small red onion, chopped

1 garlic clove, finely chopped

1 small courgette/zucchini, coarsely grated

finely grated zest and juice of 1 unwaxed lemon

2 tablespoons fruity extra virgin olive oil

First, cook the pasta for the salad in a medium pan of salted, boiling water for about 12 minutes or as per the package instructions. Drain and let cool.

In a bowl, combine the minced/ground lamb, sun-dried tomatoes, garlic, preserved lemon rind, olive oil, parsley and oregano and season well with salt and pepper.

Divide the lamb mixture into 24 even portions and cut the bocconcini into 24 equal pieces. Taking one portion of the lamb mixture, flatten it out and place one piece of bocconcini in the centre. Wrap the lamb around the cheese and roll into an even-shaped ball.

Using a heavy-based non-stick frying pan/skillet, heat enough oil for shallow frying. Fry the balls over a medium heat, rolling them around to ensure that they cook evenly. This will take about 5 minutes. Remove from the heat and place onto paper towels. Cover with a clean dish towel to keep warm.

Into the same hot frying pan/skillet place the cherry tomatoes and cook over a low heat until just warmed through.

Carefully skewer a lamb ball, followed by a tomato and a basil leaf. Repeat this sequence, finishing with a third tomato.

Combine the cold pasta with the remaining pasta salad ingredients. Be sure the pasta is cold as otherwise the mint will discolour. Mix well and season to taste.

MAKES 8 SKEWERS

LAMB MOLE WITH GREEN RICE

PRONOUNCED MOH-LEH, THIS SUMPTUOUS MEXICAN SAUCE IS MADE WITH FRESH CHILLIES/CHILES, WARMING SPICES AND DARK CHOCOLATE.

1 tablespoon groundnut/
peanut oil

4 lamb leg steaks
(approximately 125 g/
4¹/₂ oz. each)

2 red onions, finely chopped

2 green (bell) peppers, finely
sliced

2 garlic cloves, crushed

1 cinnamon stick, halved

2 dried habanero chillies/
chiles

2 teaspoons ground
coriander

2 teaspoons ground cumin

400-g/14-oz. can whole plum
tomatoes

400-g/14-oz. can red kidney
beans, rinsed and drained

25 g/1 oz. dark/bittersweet
chocolate

zest and juice of 1 lime

salt and freshly ground black
pepper

GREEN RICE

250 g/1¹/₂ cups basmati rice

zest and juice of 1 lime

200 g/5 cups baby spinach

a handful of fresh coriander/
cilantro leaves

a handful of fresh flat-leaf
parsley leaves

SERVES 4

Heat the oil in a large flameproof casserole dish. Season the lamb steaks and fry over a medium-high heat for 4–5 minutes on each side. Transfer to a plate and set aside.

Add the onions and peppers to the casserole dish and cook over a low heat for 10 minutes. Add the garlic, cinnamon, chillies/chiles, coriander, cumin, tomatoes and beans. Fill the tomato can with water and add the water to the casserole. Add the lamb, cover and simmer for 40 minutes. Stir in the chocolate, lime zest and juice.

Meanwhile put the rice in a pan with approximately 500 ml/2 cups of boiling water and simmer for 8 minutes or until cooked. Blitz the lime juice and zest with the spinach and herbs and add to the rice. Season and serve with the mole.

HARISSA PORK WITH LIME, RADISH, CARROT AND MINT SALAD

IDEAL FOR RELAXED SUMMER ENTERTAINING, AND PERFECT FOR THE BARBECUE. VERY COLOURFUL AND OH SO SIMPLE TO PREPARE.

1 unwaxed orange, segmented then roughly chopped

150 g/1 cup radishes, coarsely grated

3 organic carrots, coarsely grated

1 small red onion, finely sliced

a generous handful of fresh mint leaves, chopped

4 tablespoons fruity extra virgin olive oil

2 teaspoons red wine vinegar

juice of 1 lime

2 tablespoons pumpkin seeds

sea salt and freshly ground black pepper

HARISSA YOGURT

200 g/scant 1 cup natural/plain yogurt

4 teaspoons harissa paste

zest from 1 lime

HARISSA PORK

4–6 teaspoons harissa

2 tablespoons olive oil

4 boneless free range pork loin steaks (approximately 165 g/ 5½ oz. each)

juice of 1 lemon

sea salt and freshly ground black pepper

SERVES 4

First make the salad. Mix the orange with the radishes, carrots, red onion and mint. Mix the oil, vinegar and lime juice together with salt and pepper and pour over the salad.

Dry fry the pumpkin seeds in a non-stick frying pan/ skillet over a medium heat for 1–2 minutes, stirring continuously. Set aside.

For the harissa yogurt, mix the natural/plain yogurt, harissa and lime zest together.

For the pork, mix the harissa with the olive oil, then rub all over the meat and season with salt. Heat a griddle pan over a medium heat and fry for 3 minutes on each side, or until browned.

Transfer to serving plates. Add the lemon juice to the pan juices and reduce. Pour over the pork.

Serve the pork with the salad, harissa yogurt and toasted pumpkin seeds.

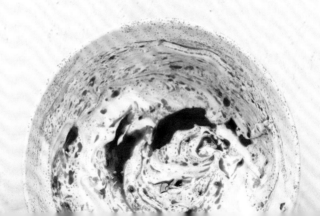

GROWING LEMONS AND LIMES

THE HISTORY OF CITRUS PLANTS IS RATHER MYSTERIOUS AND THE DIVERSITY OF VARIETIES FRANKLY MIND-BOGGLING. THEY BELONG AMONG THE OLDEST DOMESTIC PLANTS ORIGINALLY GROWN FOR DECORATION AND HEALING.

Citrus plants are evergreen trees or shrubs growing to 1–9 m (3–30 ft). The undivided leaves are usually dotted with oil glands. The bisexual flowers are large and pure white or pale pink, rich in nectar and fragrantly sweet. The sepals and petals show three- or five-fold symmetry and there are two whorls of stamens, the outer opposite the petals. A single plant can bear a great many flowers, only a very small percentage of which will develop into fruit. It is not unusual to see flowers and fruit on a citrus plant at the same time. The fruit, also known as hesperidium, is spherical or ovoid in shape and has three layers: the skin or peel, the pith and the pulp. The pulp is made of carpels filled with juice sacs containing a sweet and/or sour liquid.

After blooming, fruit development can take up to 12 months. Initially all fruits are green and do not turn yellow or orange until they ripen, but the colour change only occurs where night temperatures are relatively cool. The limes from the Caribbean and Malaysia remain green because the temperatures there (never below 15°C/60°F) do not fall sufficiently during the night. Unlike most other types of fruit, citrus fruits can stay on the tree without overripening.

In Sicily lemons are harvested using a cultivation method known as the Verdelli process. The regular harvest period runs from mid-September to May. Initially the green fruit is harvested, followed by the yellow fruits. During the summer, in order to produce a second harvest of green lemons (verdelli), very large trees are deprived of water for 35 to 60 days from June onwards, the soil is removed around the roots and all irrigation ceases. This drought causes such stress to the plants that they are forced into a second blossoming in August/September of that year. When the leaves of the lemon trees begin to dry up, the roots are covered again and the soil watered. A more concentrated second harvest can then be obtained the following summer when consumer demand for lemons is high. Unusually, the lemons often remain green but they are just as tasty and juicy.

Citrus trees respond well to grafting, pruning and other forms of growth management. When grafting, in most cases the upper tree, or scion, is one species of citrus, selected for its fruit-bearing qualities, while the lower trunk and roots, known as rootstock, are another variety chosen for hardiness and resistance to disease. The two parts are grafted by inserting a bud and a sliver of bark from the branch of the fruit-bearing tree into a T-shaped cut in the trunk of the seedling used as rootstock. The two are then bound tightly together.

Citrus fruits are more robust and less demanding than is generally assumed. The lemon, which originates from a region between the Himalayas, northern Burma and south China (a region with a temperate climate), is therefore sensitive to extremes of heat and cold, while the lime, which originates from Malaysia and is a purely tropical plant, is extremely sensitive to cold. The following growing conditions are required to ensure plants thrive in pots on patios and balconies.

Position Ideally south-facing and sheltered from wind. East- and west-facing is acceptable but north-facing or shady positions do not work. Citrus plants grown in cooler areas should be brought indoors to over-winter, ideally in a frost-free glasshouse or conservatory. Note that centrally heated rooms are too hot, with levels of light and humidity that are too low for most citrus plants.

Light Citrus plants require direct sunlight. Ensure that they are not placed too close together as they will create too much shade for each other.

Protection from the wind Citrus plants like an airy location but are very sensitive to wind and cannot cope with draughts.

Water Regularly in the growing season, ideally with rainwater, but only in the morning or early evening. Reduce the frequency of watering in winter, allowing the surface of the potting mix to dry out between each watering. Humidity of 50–60% is optimal, plus some summer rain to prevent dirt collecting on leaves. If the air is dry and warm, increase humidity by gently spraying the plants with lime-free water (avoid spraying in direct

sunlight as the leaves may burn). You can also stand potted citrus plants in trays of gravel filled with water to raise the humidity. Citrus plants require regular feeding. Following the manufacturer's instructions, use a high-nitrogen summer feed from late March to October (to encourage leaf growth) and a more balanced winter feed from late October to late March (to help develop flowers and fruits).

Temperature Optimal growing is in the range 15–30°C (59–86°F). Generally, when growing citrus plants, temperatures should never drop below 5–7°C (41–45°F), as the plants cease growing at about 12°C (54°F). Ideally, lemons and limes require a minimum temperature of 10°C (50°F), although Meyer's lemon (C. x limon 'Meyer') can survive temperatures down to 5°C (41°F). Temperatures should not climb beyond 30°C (86°F), as this will also stop growth. Never stand a citrus plant outside until after the last cold snap in spring, as late frosts can cause young shoots to freeze and die.

STEAK AND POLENTA CHIPS WITH LEMON PARSLEY PESTO

ELEGANT BUT VERY STRAIGHTFORWARD. POLENTA TREATED WELL IS UTTERLY DIVINE. IT SHOULD ALWAYS BE IN YOUR PANTRY.

30 g/1½ tablespoons unsalted butter

100g/⅔ cup quick-cook polenta

zest of 1 lemon

25 g/⅓ cup freshly grated Parmesan cheese

4 x 200 g/7 oz. sirloin steaks, 1–2-cm/ ½–¾-in. thick

1 tablespoon groundnut/ peanut oil, plus extra for deep frying

1¾ tablespoons 'oo' Italian flour, to coat

1 egg, beaten

40 g/¾ cup panko crumbs

sea salt and freshly ground black pepper

LEMON PARSLEY PESTO

a handful of rocket/arugula

2 handfuls of flat-leaf parsley

10 g/⅓ oz. pine nuts

10 g/⅛ cup freshly grated Parmesan cheese

2 garlic cloves

zest and juice of 1 unwaxed lemon

4 tablespoons olive oil

SERVES 4

First prepare the polenta. Bring 400 ml/1⅔ cups salted water to the boil and add a third of the butter. Slowly add the polenta, stirring continuously. Add the lemon zest. Cover and let rest for 20 minutes. Add another third of the butter, cheese, salt and pepper. Transfer the polenta to a greased baking pan and spread to a thickness of 1.5 cm/½ in.

To make the pesto, combine the ingredients in a pestle and mortar or blend in food processor. Season to taste with salt and pepper.

Cut the steak lengthways into four strips and season with salt. Heat a frying pan/skillet over high heat, add the groundnut/peanut oil and the remaining butter, then cook the steaks for 2–3 minutes on each side, depending on the thickness, until brown and medium rare. Rest in a warm place for 8–10 minutes, while you cook the chips/fries.

To make the polenta chips/fries, cut the polenta into small slices about 2.5 x 10 cm/1 x 4 in. Put the flour, egg and panko crumbs into three separate bowls ready to coat the chips/fries.

Heat the oil in a deep heavy pan to 200°C/400°F. Dredge the chips/fries in the flour, then dip in the egg and then dip in the panko crumbs. Deep fry in batches until golden brown, about 2 minutes. Drain on a wire rack with paper towels underneath to catch any excess oil.

Serve the steaks with the chips/fries and pesto.

MEXICAN CHIPOTLE TURKEY TOSTADAS

TURKEY CAN MAKE A WELCOME CHANGE FROM CHICKEN AND SOMEHOW COPES BETTER WITH STRONG FLAVOURS OF LIME AND CHIPOTLE. THIS IS IDEAL FOR A HUNGRY GATHERING. SERVE WITH FRESH TOMATO SALSA.

1 red onion, finely sliced

1 tablespoon maple syrup

zest of 2 and juice of 4 limes, plus extra wedges to serve

1 kg/2¼ lbs. turkey fillets

90 g/½ cup chipotle paste

1 tablespoon barbecue sauce

½ tablespoon vegetable oil

a generous handful of coriander/cilantro, stalks finely chopped, leaves torn

2 tablespoons groundnut/ peanut oil

3 large tortilla wraps, quartered

75 g/⅔ cup crumbled feta cheese

sea salt and freshly ground black pepper

TOMATO SALSA

4 medium tomatoes, skinned and deseeded

½ red onion

1 garlic clove

1 tablespoon olive oil

1 tablespoon lemon juice

sea salt and freshly ground pepper

a baking sheet lined with baking foil

SERVES 4

To make the tomato salsa, mix all of the ingredients together in a bowl. Season and set aside.

Preheat the grill/broiler to high.

Cover the red onion with boiling water for 15 seconds. Drain well, then mix with the maple syrup, juice of 2 limes and a pinch of sea salt. Cover and chill.

Season the turkey and mix with the chipotle paste, barbecue sauce, zest and juice of 2 limes, ½ tablespoon vegetable oil and the coriander/cilantro stalks. Lay the turkey on the prepared baking sheet and grill/broil under the preheated grill/broiler for 5–7 minutes on each side until charred and cooked through.

Meanwhile heat the groundnut oil in a small non-stick frying pan/skillet and fry the tortilla pieces in batches over a medium heat for 30 seconds on each side until crisp. Drain on paper towels.

Slice the turkey and divide between the tortilla pieces. Top each with a little crumbled feta, red onion mixture and a few coriander/cilantro leaves. Serve with a wedge of lime and a spoonful of tomato salsa.

TANDOORI LAMB CUTLETS WITH TOMATO AND CORIANDER SALSA

TANDOORI IS NORTHERN INDIAN AND RELIES ON SPICES AND YOGURT. COLOURFUL AND STRAIGHTFORWARD, THIS DISH IS IDEAL FOR RELAXED ENTERTAINING. SERVE WITH POPPADOMS AND LIME PICKLE.

150 g/³⁄₄ cup basmati rice

75 g/¹⁄₃ cup tandoori paste

75 g/¹⁄₄ cup Greek-style yogurt

1 tablespoon freshly squeezed lemon juice

1 tablespoon zest from unwaxed lemon

12 French trimmed lamb cutlets (approximately 600 g/1 lb. 6 oz.)

TOMATO AND CORIANDER SALSA

200 g/1¹⁄₃ cups cherry tomatoes, halved

1 small red onion, finely chopped

zest of 1 lemon

2 tablespoons freshly chopped coriander/cilantro leaves

sea salt and freshly ground black pepper

SERVES 4

Cook the rice according to the package instructions.

Preheat the grill or barbecue to high.

Combine the tandoori paste, yogurt, lemon juice and zest in a large bowl. Add the lamb and turn to coat the lamb in the mixture. Season.

Cook the lamb on a heated grill or barbecue for 4 minutes each side, or until browned and cooked as desired. Allow to stand for 5 minutes.

To make the tomato and coriander/cilantro salsa, simply combine all the ingredients in a bowl and season to taste with salt and pepper.

Serve the lamb with the rice and salsa.

FIVE-SPICE PORK FILLET

WITHOUT THE LIME ZEST AND JUICE THIS PORK MIGHT BE REALLY RATHER ORDINARY. BE SURE TO USE UNWAXED LIMES FOR MAXIMUM FLAVOUR IMPACT. THIS DISH IS REALLY COLOURFUL AND STRAIGHTFORWARD TO PREPARE.

2 shallots, thinly sliced

2 garlic cloves, thinly sliced

2 firm pears, cut into 6 wedges

4-cm/1 ½-in. piece of fresh ginger, peeled, cut into matchsticks

2 tablespoons brown sugar

2 tablespoons tamari soy sauce

3 teaspoons Chinese five-spice powder

4 tablespoons olive oil

zest and juice of 2 limes

800 g/1¾ lbs. pork fillet, trimmed

3 tablespoons sesame seeds

100 g/⅔ cup yellow beans

100 g/⅔ cup green beans

a roasting pan lined with parchment paper

SERVES 4

Preheat the oven to 180°C (350°F) Gas 4.

Place the shallots, garlic, pears, ginger, sugar, tamari and five-spice powder in the prepared roasting pan, drizzle with 2 tablespoons of the oil and toss to combine. Roast in the preheated oven for 20 minutes or until the pears are just soft. Add the lime juice.

Meanwhile, rub the pork with 2 teaspoons of oil and lime zest, and roll in the sesame seeds. Heat the remaining oil in a flameproof casserole and cook the pork until brown on all sides. Transfer the pan to the oven and roast the pork for 15 minutes, or until just cooked through. Cover the pork with foil and rest for 5 minutes.

Bring a pan of salted water to the boil, add the beans and cook until tender. Slice the spiced pork and serve with the roasted pear mixture and beans.

PORK ESCALOPES WITH LEMON SAUCE

THIS IS A GREAT RECIPE FOR YOUNG ADULTS TO MAKE AND FEEL PROUD.
MY DAUGHTER LOVES PORK AND CHICKEN TREATED THIS WAY, AND SO
DOES MY ALWAYS READY-TO-EAT HUSBAND.

4 pieces pork loin, 150-g/
5 oz. each

100 g/2 cups sourdough
breadcrumbs or spelt bread

zest of 2 lemons

2 sprigs fresh rosemary,
finely chopped

4 fresh sage leaves

100 ml/scant ½ cup milk

2 eggs

50 g/½ cup 'oo' Italian
plain/all-purpose flour

100 g/1 stick minus
1 tablespoon unsalted
butter

2 tablespoons olive oil

freshly squeezed juice of
2 lemons

120 ml/½ cup dry white wine

lemon wedges, to serve

sea salt and freshly ground
black pepper

SERVES 4

Cut off any excess fat from the pork, then wrap the slices in clingfilm/
plastic wrap and bash with a rolling pin until they are about 5-mm/
¼-in. thick.

Place the breadcrumbs in a bowl and add the grated lemon zest. Add
the rosemary and sage and season with salt and pepper.

Mix the milk and eggs together in a bowl. Place the flour in a separate
bowl, add a small pinch of salt and mix together.

Pat one of the pork escalopes in the flour. Next, dip the pork in the egg
mixture, then coat in the breadcrumbs. Dip and coat the pork a second
time so that it is really well covered in crumbs. Do the same with the rest
of the pork.

Heat a large non-stick frying pan/skillet over medium heat and melt
half the butter with the olive oil. When the butter is foaming, add the
escalopes and fry them for about 6 minutes on each side, until golden
brown. Drain on paper towels and keep warm.

To make the sauce add the remaining butter to a medium-sized saucepan
with the lemon juice and wine. Turn up the heat and let bubble until the
sauce has reduced by half. Serve the pork with a wedge of lemon and
the sauce on the side.

FISH
AND
SEAFOOD

MUSSELS WITH SAMPHIRE

I ADORE THE FLAVOUR AND COLOUR CONTRAST IN THIS RECIPE.
STRINGLESS GREEN TIPS OF SAMPHIRE ARE BEST.

4 handfuls of samphire tips

200 ml/scant 1 cup dry white wine

2 small shallots, finely chopped

about 1 kg/2¼ lbs. mussels, debearded and cleaned

2 garlic cloves, crushed

a generous pinch of saffron

250 ml/1 cup sour cream

a generous handful of fresh flat-leaf parsley, finely chopped

zest and juice of 2 unwaxed lemons

2 medium-sized leeks, cut into matchsticks

2 small organic carrots, cut into matchsticks

sea salt and freshly ground black pepper

SERVES 4

Bring a pan of water to the boil and prepare a separate bowl of ice water. Add the samphire to the boiling water, cook for 1 minute or until tender, then plunge into the ice water.

Place the wine and chopped shallots in a pan and bring to the boil. Add the mussels and the garlic. Cover and leave for 3 minutes until the mussels are open. Discard any unopened mussels.

Remove all the mussels from the pot. Take the meat out of the shells, leaving 4 mussels in their shells. Put the meat back in the pan. Add the saffron, cream, parsley, lemon zest and juice. Season.

Place the samphire in the bowl with the reserved mussels in the shell. Spoon over the mussel broth, and leek and carrot to garnish.

Serve with plenty of crusty bread to mop up the juices.

SPAGHETTINI WITH CALAMARI, ROSEMARY AND LEMON

THIS IS A LIGHT AND FRESH-TASTING PASTA DISH. TAKE CALAMARI, ADD A LITTLE CHILLI/CHILE HEAT AND AROMATIC ROSEMARY AND LIFT THE WHOLE DISH WITH TANGY LEMON ZEST AND JUICE.

4 tablespoons extra virgin olive oil

1 onion, finely diced

500 g/1¼ lbs. cleaned calamari, cut into 2-cm/ ¾-in. pieces

1 tablespoon chopped fresh rosemary leaves

3 garlic cloves, very thinly sliced

2 long red chillies/chiles, thinly sliced

finely grated rind and juice of 1 lemon

400 g/4 cups dried spaghettini or 300 g/3 cups fresh spaghettini

lemon wedges, to serve

salt and freshly ground black pepper

TOASTED CRUMBS

70 g/1½ cups coarse fresh sourdough breadcrumbs

3½ tablespoons olive oil

1 garlic clove, crushed

SERVES 4

Heat a medium saucepan over a medium heat. Add the olive oil and onion and stir occasionally until the onion starts to caramelize (10–15 minutes). Increase the heat to high, add the calamari, rosemary, garlic and chillies/chiles and toss occasionally until the calamari is just cooked (1–2 minutes). Remove from the heat, add the lemon rind and juice and season to taste.

Meanwhile, to make the toasted crumbs, combine the ingredients in a non-stick frying pan/skillet over medium-high heat and stir until crisp (5–10 minutes). Set aside.

Cook the spaghettini in a large saucepan of boiling salted water until al dente (8–10 minutes for dried, 3–4 minutes for fresh). Drain, reserving a little cooking water, toss with the calamari and reserved water and mix until the pasta is well coated.

Serve hot, sprinkled with the toasted breadcrumbs, with lemon wedges to the side.

SALMON ESCABECHE WITH CELERY AND CITRUS

A TRUE MARRIAGE MADE IN HEAVEN. I ADORE FENNEL, CELERY AND FISH, AND COULD EAT IT EVERY DAY, NONSTOP. ESCABECHE IS A SPANISH METHOD OF SEARING FISH OR MEAT AND THEN MARINATING IT IN A TANGY CITRUS DRESSING. DO TRY WITH OTHER FISH – MACKEREL IS DIVINE.

2 tablespoons olive oil

4 boneless salmon fillets, skinned

2 shallots, sliced into thin rounds

2 fennel bulbs, trimmed and thinly sliced, reserve the fronds to garnish

4 celery stalks, as white as possible, finely sliced

3 fresh bay leaves

4 garlic cloves, thinly sliced

zest of 2 lemons and juice of 1

zest of 2 limes and juice of 1

a handful of fresh mint leaves

salt and freshly ground black pepper

SERVES 4

Heat the oil in a large non-stick frying pan/skillet. Season the salmon fillets with salt and fry over a medium heat for 3 minutes on each side until a little opaque. Set aside to rest.

Return the pan to the heat. Add the shallots, fennel, celery and bay leaves. Season and cook for 5 minutes. Add the garlic and cook for a further 2 minutes. Remove from the heat. Now add the citrus juice and zest along with 4 tablespoons of water.

Add the fish to this citrus mixture and spoon the juices to coat the fish. Arrange on a platter with the mint leaves and fennel fronds, and serve with crusty bread to mop up the juices.

MONKFISH AND BAY LEAF SKEWERS WITH LEMON AND VEGETABLE SLAW

IDEAL FOR RELAXED ENTERTAINING, YOU CAN EITHER COOK THESE ON THE BARBECUE OR UNDER THE GRILL/BROILER. BAY LEAVES, FISH AND LEMON ARE A FLAVOUR-MATCH MADE IN HEAVEN. I RECOMMEND FORGING A GOOD RELATIONSHIP WITH YOUR FISHMONGER – THEY CAN SKIN THE MONKFISH FOR YOU.

VEGETABLE SLAW

2 red apples

2 medium carrots, peeled

300 g/2 cups celeriac, peeled and grated

200 g/2 cups Savoy cabbage, finely shredded

a handful of fresh flat-leaf parsley, finely chopped

a handful of fresh chives, finely chopped

40 g/$\frac{1}{3}$ cup pecans, roasted and roughly chopped

5 tablespoons buttermilk

5 tablespoons extra virgin olive oil

grated zest from 1 unwaxed lemon, plus juice from $\frac{1}{2}$

SKEWERS

1 kg/2$\frac{1}{4}$ lbs. monkfish tails, skinned

24 large fresh bay leaves

olive oil, for brushing

lemon wedges, to serve

sea salt and freshly ground black pepper

8 bamboo barbecue skewers, soaked in cold water

SERVES 4

To make the vegetable slaw, cut the apples and the carrots into small, slim matchsticks. Place the sliced vegetables in a large bowl with the grated celeriac, shredded cabbage, fresh herbs and chopped pecans.

In a separate bowl combine the buttermilk, olive oil, lemon zest and juice. Season to taste with salt and pepper and stir together. Pour onto the vegetables and toss to mix. Set the slaw aside in the refrigerator until ready to serve.

Cut the monkfish tails into 16 even-sized pieces of around 5 cm/2 in. each. Thread three bay leaves and two pieces of monkfish alternately onto each of the pre-soaked bamboo skewers, starting and ending with a bay leaf. Brush the fish with olive oil and season with salt and pepper.

Preheat a barbecue or grill/broiler to medium. Cook the skewers on/under the heat for 2 minutes on each side until the fish is cooked through. Serve with the slaw and lemon wedges to squeeze over.

MASHED BEETROOT AND HORSERADISH WITH MACKEREL

A COLOURFUL, SIMPLE AND TOTALLY DIVINE DISH, BUT DO MAKE SURE THAT YOUR MACKEREL IS SUPER FRESH.

8 medium beetroot/beets

4 x 175-g/6-oz. mackerel fillets

50 g/3½ tablespoons unsalted butter

4 tablespoons fresh horseradish, finely grated

zest and juice of 2 lemons, plus 1 for garnish

a handful of fresh flat-leaf parsley leaves, chopped

sea salt and freshly ground black pepper

SERVES 4

Preheat the oven to 180°C (350°F) Gas 4.

Place the beetroot/beets on a baking sheet and roast for about 25 minutes or until tender. Peel while hot.

Heat a griddle pan to hot. Brush the mackerel fillets with butter and cook skin-side down for about 4 minutes, depending on their size. Flip and cook for a further 2 minutes on the other side, then remove them from the heat and allow to rest.

Roughly mash the beetroot/beets with the horseradish. Add the zest and juice of the lemons and a handful of flat-leaf parsley. Season to taste with salt and pepper.

Serve the mash with mackerel and lemon wedges.

SEABASS WITH ROASTED RED PEPPER BUTTER, BASIL AND OLIVES

WHY NOT BARBECUE ALL YEAR ROUND? IT'S SUCH A CONVENIENT WAY TO COOK.

1 whole sea bass or sea
  bream, gutted

1 lemon, cut into wedges

leaves from a small bunch
  of fresh basil

120 ml/½ cup white wine

12 black or kalamata olives

sea salt and freshly ground
  pepper

RED PEPPER BUTTER

2 red (bell) peppers

25 g/¼ stick unsalted butter

1 garlic clove

SERVES 2-4

Preheat the oven to 180°C (350°F) Gas 4.

To make the red (bell) pepper butter, roast the peppers in the preheated oven for 35 minutes. Remove from the oven and skin and deseed the peppers. Place the pepper flesh, butter and garlic in a food processor and blend together until you have a smooth paste.

Preheat the barbecue/griddle to medium.

Wash the fish and trim the fins with kitchen scissors. On both sides of the fish make vertical incisions to the bone. Place the lemon wedges into the incisions. Smear the red pepper butter all over the fish and place the basil leaves into the cavity. Place the fish onto a double thickness, large sheet of foil. Lift the sides of the foil slightly to make a parcel. Add the wine and olives and season with salt and pepper. Seal the foil.

Cook for 30 minutes on the preheated barbecue/griddle. Insert a metal skewer into the fish and hold it there for a few seconds. Press the skewer against the back of your hand. If it feels warm, the fish is done. Serve.

PICKLING AND PRESERVING

IF YOU WISH TO TAKE THE FLAVOURS OF LEMONS AND LIMES TO A DEEPER LEVEL AND TO ADD A UNIQUE, INTENSE AND IRRESISTIBLE COMPLEXITY TO OTHERWISE SIMPLE DISHES, LEMONS OR LIMES WHICH HAVE BEEN PRESERVED IN SEA SALT ARE THE ANSWER. HERE I'VE GIVEN A SIMPLE PRESERVING METHOD THAT YOU CAN FOLLOW AT HOME.

Preserved lemons or limes add a fermented quality to dishes that fresh fruit cannot match. They add a big punch of flavour: heavy citrus, heavy floral notes from the essential oils in the peel, and ultimately heavy umami. It's that extra something in the background of a dish that elevates it from ordinary to extraordinary.

For generations, preserves and pickles have epitomized the values at the heart of a well-run, contented kitchen. In a generation of renewed frugality, they are enjoying a renaissance. Preserves and pickles embody and thrive on seasonal abundance. They waste not, so we want not and they quite literally save the best of the season in jars. More than that, preserving evokes deep-rooted, almost primeval feelings of self-sufficiency and the history of preserved lemons and limes can be traced back through many cultures and thousands of years.

An actual recipe surfaces in the 12th-century Egyptian treatise, On Lemon, Its Drinking and Use, by the Arabic-speaking court physician Ibn Jumay. Jumay's recipe, now some nine centuries old, is – almost exactly – the recipe of today. Over the past thousand years, these salt-cured fruits have made a meandering journey north and west, joining the cuisines of Israel, Iran, Turkey and India. But it wasn't until far more recently that they began to appear in English-language cookbooks. And yet, despite their ancient roots, they have retained their aura of exoticism and remain a new discovery for many home cooks.

Preserved lemons and limes also have a strong association with Middle Eastern and North African cuisines and their unique zesty, salty yet mellow flavour permeates many of the traditional meat and couscous dishes. Strips of preserved lemon or lime can also be added to salads, soups and dressings, or mixed with olives and other appetizers. Swap out regular lemons for preserved ones in your go-to recipes for roast chicken and fish or grilled meats. For an easy week-night meal, toss pasta with some good olive oil, a little garlic and some chopped preserved lemon peel. Mix a little of the zesty preserving liquid into a Bloody Mary cocktail or swirl chopped peel into yogurt with a little honey. Use preserved lemons and limes to liven up potato or grain salads, and to enhance hummus or even guacamole. You can even freeze and then grate the peel for granita!

Preserved lemons or lime are exceptionally easy to prepare – see the method on the right.

PRESERVED LEMONS AND LIMES

Preserved lemons are an essential ingredient in several recipes in this book and in my North African dishes. Preserving has a long history as a way of contributing supremely intense flavour. In times gone by, preserving was the best way to enjoy lemons, for both their nutrition and flavour. Preserved lemons work extremely well with turmeric and coriander (cilantro), and in fish and chicken dishes and the preserving juices can also be used in salad dressings.

3 lemons
3 limes (or all lemons if preferred)
6 tablespoons sea salt
Juice of 3 lemons and 2 limes
2 tablespoons olive oil
750-ml (1^1/$_2$-pint) jar with a rubber seal, sterilized

Wash and scrub the lemons and limes. Quarter each lemon and lime from the top to within 1.5 cm (^{3}/$_4$ in.) of the stem so that the sections are still attached. Carefully open out each lemon and lime and sprinkle each with about 1 teaspoon sea salt, then close up and reshape the fruit.

Put 1^1/$_2$ tablespoons sea salt in the bottom of the sterilized jar. Pack in the lemon and limes, pushing them down well. Sprinkle with more salt. Leave the jar to stand in a warm kitchen for 4–5 days for the juices to be drawn out.

Press the fruit down again as much as you can and pour in enough lemon juice to cover. Seal with a layer of olive oil. Close the jar and leave to ripen for 1 month in a cool place and use within 1 year. There is no need to refrigerate after opening.

POMEGRANATE-GLAZED SALMON WITH LEMON CAULIFLOWER MASH

OUR NEIGHBOUR AND FRIEND RECENTLY RETURNED FROM A TRIP TO ICELAND SPECIFICALLY TO FISH FOR SALMON. NEEDLESS TO SAY AN ENORMOUS SALMON ARRIVED BACK WITH HIM AS A GIFT FOR US. I SOON SET TO WORK TO DREAM UP AN EXCELLENT TREATMENT FOR THIS MAGNIFICENT FISH THAT IS SO WHOLESOME AND WONDERFUL. I HOPE YOU ENJOY THE OUTCOME.

600 g/4¾ cups cauliflower florets

2 garlic cloves

zest of 2 lemons and 1 tablespoon juice

2 tablespoons olive oil

4 salmon fillets, skinned

2½ tablespoons pomegranate molasses

100 g/⅔ cup pomegranate seeds

sea salt and freshly ground black pepper

a handful of fresh mint leaves, to serve

lemon wedges, to serve

SERVES 4

Bring a pan of salted water to the boil and add the cauliflower florets. Cook on a rolling boiling until tender. Drain.

Mix the garlic, lemon zest and juice and 1 tablespoon olive oil together and mash through the cauliflower. Keep warm.

Season the salmon fillets, coat with the remaining oil and fry in a non-stick frying pan/skillet over a high heat for 6–8 minutes on both sides until crisp. Pour over the pomegranate molasses and pomegranate seeds. Allow to bubble for 1 minute, then take off the heat.

Serve the salmon with the mash and glaze. Add mint leaves to garnish and a wedge of lemon to the side for squeezing.

HALIBUT WITH PRESERVED LEMON SAUCE

SUCH A DELICIOUS FIRM FLESH FISH THAT MARRIES SO WELL WITH PRESERVED LEMON. BE SURE TO ENJOY WITH STUNNING RIPE AND SWEET TOMATOES.

4 x 165-g/5½-oz. halibut steaks, skin on

1 tablespoon olive oil

sea salt and freshly ground black pepper

lemon wedges, to serve

PRESERVED LEMON SAUCE

2 preserved lemons (see page 101)

a handful of fresh mint leaves

a handful of fresh basil leaves

a squeeze of lemon juice

175 ml/¾ cup crème fraîche or sour cream

SERVES 4

First make the preserved lemon sauce. Cut the preserved lemons into quarters and rinse under cold running water, removing and discarding the flesh. You only need the peel. Blend the peel along with the herbs and 3 tablespoons water to a smooth purée in a small food processor. Adjust the seasoning and stir in the crème fraîche. Cover and set aside.

Preheat the oven to 150°C (300°F) Gas 2.

Over a medium heat add the oil to a medium non-stick ovenproof frying pan/skillet. Season the fish with salt and pepper. Once the pan is hot lay the fish in skin-side down and cook, without touching, for about 2 minutes. Place the pan in the oven and cook for a further 4 minutes.

Remove the pan from the oven. Carefully lift the fish onto serving plates. Spoon over the preserved lemon sauce and serve with wilted spinach and lemon wedges on the side for squeezing.

LOBSTER TAILS WITH LIME BUTTER

THIS IS A RECIPE FOR A SPECIAL OCCASION. I RECOMMEND MAKING
FRIENDS WITH YOUR FISHMONGER WHO CAN CUT THE TAILS IN HALF.

5 tablespoons lime juice

150 g/1¼ sticks unsalted
butter

2 raw large lobster tails,
cut in half

1 tablespoon olive oil

sea salt and freshly
ground black pepper

2 limes cut into wedges,
to serve

SERVES 4

Preheat the oven to 200°C (400°F) Gas 6. Warm
a baking sheet in the oven.

Heat the lime juice in a medium-sized saucepan.
Add the butter and whisk to form a sauce.

Season the lobster tails. Heat the oil in a large
frying pan/skillet and fry the lobster tails for
3 minutes. Transfer them to the hot baking sheet,
drizzle with lime butter and roast for 10 minutes
until the flesh is opaque. Serve with lime wedges.

KING PRAWNS/JUMBO SHRIMP

FRESH, VIBRANT AND A WINNING COMBINATION OF BALANCED FLAVOURS,
THIS ZINGY DISH MAKES A REAL CROWD-PLEASER AS AN APPETIZER.

2 tablespoons
groundnut/peanut oil

1 garlic clove, chopped

1 red chilli/chile,
deseeded and sliced

4 teaspoons finely
chopped fresh ginger

400 ml/1²⁄₃ cups chicken
stock

2 tablespoons tamari soy
sauce

a dash of Thai fish sauce

400 g/14 oz. raw king
prawns/jumbo shrimp,
peeled and deveined

100 g/²⁄₃ cup mangetout/
snowpeas, cut into
strips

2 tablespoons lime juice

a handful of fresh
coriander/cilantro
leaves, chopped

4 spring onions/
scallions, finely
chopped

1 lime cut into wedges,
to serve

SERVES 4

Heat the groundnut/peanut oil, ideally in a wok
or large, deep non-stick frying pan/skillet. Fry the
garlic, chilli/chile and ginger until they are starting
to soften but still retain some bite; about 2 minutes.

Add the chicken stock, tamari soy sauce and fish
sauce and bring to the boil.

Add the king prawns/jumbo shrimp to the boiling
stock and stir well. Add the mangetout/snowpeas
and simmer for 3 minutes or until the prawns/
shrimp are pink and cooked through. Remove from
the heat and stir through the lime juice, coriander/
cilantro and spring onions/scallions. Serve
immediately with wedges of lime for squeezing.

MONKFISH AND ASPARAGUS RISOTTO WITH LEMON THYME BUTTER

DO USE THE TAIL OF THE MONKFISH FOR THE DISH AND ASK YOUR FISHMONGER TO REMOVE THE MEMBRANE FROM THE TAIL AS THIS CAN BE A BIT TRICKY. THIS IS POPULAR WITH MY FAMILY AND HUSBAND WHO HAVE AN AVERSION TO FISH BONES.

750 ml/3 cups vegetable stock

8 new-season asparagus spears, sliced diagonally, reserve the woody stems for the broth

1$\frac{1}{2}$ tablespoons olive oil

50 g/3$\frac{1}{2}$ tablespoons unsalted butter

4 shallots, finely chopped

225 g/1$\frac{1}{8}$ cups carnaroli rice

600 g/1 lb. 6 oz. monkfish tail (see recipe introduction)

fresh lemon thyme leaves, to garnish

LEMON THYME BUTTER

50 g/3$\frac{1}{2}$ tablespoons unsalted butter, softened

a generous handful of fresh lemon thyme leaves, roughly chopped

1 small garlic clove, finely chopped

zest of 1 unwaxed lemon

a baking sheet lined with parchment paper

SERVES 4

Preheat the oven to 180°C (350°F) Gas 4.

To make the lemon thyme butter, mix the ingredients together and wrap in clingfilm/plastic wrap. Chill until firm.

Heat the stock in a pan and add the woody asparagus stems.

In a wide-based pan, heat the oil and butter and sweat the shallots until golden. Now add the rice and continue to stir for 2 minutes. Start adding a ladle of stock at a time to the rice and stir well between each addition. Repeat this process until the rice is al dente, then stir in the asparagus spears.

Meanwhile, season the monkfish tails and place them on the prepared baking sheet. Add some of the thyme butter on top and bake in the preheated oven for 12 minutes.

When the risotto is cooked (this should be after approximately 15 minutes) add the sliced monkfish tail and stir once gently. Spoon into warmed shallow serving bowls and top with the remaining lemon thyme butter. Scatter with some fresh thyme leaves and serve.

ROASTED HAKE, WHITE BEANS AND PADRON PEPPERS

THE PADRON PEPPERS AND SPICY CHORIZO COMPLEMENT THE HAKE MAGNIFICENTLY AND CREATE A TRULY TASTY SPANISH DISH, IDEAL FOR ANY INFORMAL SUPPER PARTY.

3 tablespoons olive oil

4 shallots, finely diced

1 medium red chilli/chile, sliced

100 g/⅔ cup dried haricot or cannellini beans, soaked overnight with fresh bay leaves and garlic

3 tablespoons white wine

500 ml/generous 2 cups chicken stock

4 x hake fillets (weighing about 170 g/6 oz.), skin on

75 g/3 oz. padron peppers

80 g/⅔ cup diced chorizo

a generous bunch of fresh flat-leaf parsley, chopped

zest and juice of 2 lemons

30 g/¼ stick unsalted butter

2 garlic cloves, crushed

sea salt and freshly ground black pepper

SERVES 4

Heat 1 tablespoon of olive oil in a medium non-stick frying pan/skillet. Add the shallots and chilli/chile and cook over a medium heat. Add the drained soaked beans and white wine and reduce by half. Then add the chicken stock and cook for 45 minutes until the beans are tender. Add more liquid if necessary. Season with salt and pepper.

Heat a heavy-based frying pan/skillet and add 1 tablespoon olive oil. Season the hake with salt and pepper and place skin-side down in the pan. Cook for about 4 minutes, until the skin is crispy. Turn and cook for a further 3 minutes. Cover the pan with foil.

Heat the remaining olive oil in a second pan. Add the padron peppers, chorizo, parsley, lemon zest and juice, butter and garlic. Cook for about 2 minutes until the peppers are wilted.

When ready to serve, spoon the cooked beans onto the middle of a warmed plate. Top with hake and spoon over the padron peppers and chorizo. Serve with plenty of crusty bread for mopping up the juices.

VEGETABLE SIDES

ROAST CAULIFLOWER WITH ALMONDS AND PRESERVED LEMON

THIS RECIPE WAS BORN OUT OF A DESIRE TO EAT QUICKLY, HEALTHILY, AND OF COURSE, TASTILY.

1 large cauliflower, cut into bite-sized florets

115 g/1 cup whole almonds

1 medium red chilli/chile, deseeded and finely chopped

3 tablespoons fruity extra virgin olive oil

1 preserved lemon, finely chopped (see page 101)

a handful of fresh flat-leaf parsley leaves

seeds from 1 whole pomegranate

sea salt and freshly ground black pepper

SERVES 4

Preheat the oven to 200°c (400°F) Gas 6.

Put the cauliflower florets on a baking sheet, drizzle over 1 tablespoon extra virgin olive oil and bake in the preheated oven for 30 minutes until the cauliflower is brown and crispy at the edges. Remove from the oven and set aside.

Toast the whole almonds on a baking sheet for 6 minutes. Remove from the oven and let cool. Coarsely chop and set aside.

Arrange the cauliflower florets on a platter.

Mix the chilli/chile, the remaining extra virgin olive oil, the chopped preserved lemon and seasoning together in a bowl. Pour the dressing over the cauliflower and add the parsley, toasted almonds and pomegranate seeds. Serve and enjoy.

THREE BEANS WITH MINT AND LIMES

THIS IS GOOD SERVED WITH FISH OR MEAT. IT'S EXTRA SPECIAL IF THE BEANS ARE HOME GROWN AS THERE IS SO MUCH PLEASURE IN GROWING YOUR OWN.

175 g/1 cup broad/fava beans, shelled

150 g/1 cup runner beans

150 g/1 cup French beans

1 small red onion, finely chopped

zest and juice of 2 limes

2 tablespoons fruity extra virgin olive oil

a generous handful of fresh mint leaves, roughly chopped

sea salt and freshly ground black pepper

SERVES 4

Cook all the beans together in a pan of salted, boiling water, until al-dente – approximately 4 minutes. Drain and refresh with cold water.

Dress the beans with the onion and lime zest. Mix the oil and lime juice together in a small bowl. Add the salt and pepper. Pour over when ready to serve and scatter over the mint. Adjust the lime juice and oil to suit your tastebuds.

LEMON AND PARSLEY MASH

THIS IS TOTALLY IDEAL WITH FISH AS AN ACCOMPANIMENT OR TO LAY THE FISH ON TOP. IT'S ELEGANT, REALLY TASTY AND RATHER SIMPLE TO PREPARE. I HEAVILY ENDORSE BAKING THE POTATOES IN THEIR SKINS.

1 kg/2¼ lbs. Maris Piper, King Edward, Desiree, Pentland Crown or Rooster potatoes, unpeeled

a very generous handful of fresh flat-leaf parsley, finely chopped

zest of 2 unwaxed lemons, and freshly squeezed juice of 1

100 g/7 tablespoons unsalted butter

100 ml/scant ½ cup plus 1 tablespoon single/ light cream

sea salt and freshly ground black pepper

SERVES 4

Preheat the oven to 180°C (350°F) Gas 4.

Prick each of the potatoes a few times with a fork. Arrange directly on the oven shelf and bake for about 30–40 minutes, until they are tender when a knife point is inserted into the centre.

When cool enough to handle, cut each potato in half. Scoop out the flesh and place in a potato ricer (if you have one) with a bowl underneath. (Alternatively mash in a bowl with a masher.) Beat in all the remaining ingredients, season to taste with salt and pepper and serve warm.

STEAMED ASPARAGUS WITH SAFFRON LIME AIOLI

THE ASPARAGUS I GROW ON MY PLOT IS SUCH A HIGHLIGHT FOR ME EACH YEAR. I AM ALWAYS THRILLED. MY NEIGHBOUR, DAVID GEER, GROWS A BUMPER CROP AND, I FEAR, I MIGHT NEVER HAVE SUCH SPLENDID ASPARAGUS AS HIS. THANK YOU, DAVID, FOR YOUR MARVELLOUS ASPARAGUS. THIS IS ANOTHER SIMPLE SIDE DISH OR STARTER. TASTY AND VISUALLY STUNNING.

1 kg/2¼ lbs. fresh asparagus, thick stalks removed

1 whole egg and 1 egg yolk

1 teaspoon French mustard

½ teaspoon granulated sugar

1 garlic clove

150 ml/⅔ cup olive oil

2 generous pinches of saffron, soaked in 1 tablespoon white wine vinegar

zest of 1 lime

1 tablespoon lime juice

a handful of freshly snipped chives, to garnish

sea salt and freshly ground black pepper

SERVES 4

Steam the asparagus until tender and refresh with cold water to retain its lovely bright colour.

To make the aïoli, put the egg and egg yolk, mustard, salt, pepper, sugar and garlic into a food processor and whizz, adding the oil little by little until you have a thick mayonnaise.

In a small pan warm the saffron and vinegar mixture with lime juice and zest to soften. Cool, then whizz into the mayonnaise.

Serve with the asparagus and snipped chives on top.

HEALTH BENEFITS

LEMONS POSSESS BRIGHT, BOLD, ZESTY BRILLIANCE AND VERSATILITY WHICH EXTEND FAR BEYOND THE KITCHEN AND INTO THE REALMS OF HEALTH AND WELL BEING. LEMONS AND OTHER CITRUS FRUITS ARE CALLED INTO SERVICE AS PREVENTIONS, REMEMDIES AND SOMETIMES EVEN CURES FOR MINOR AND SOME MAJOR AILMENTS.

When the zest and juice are combined with warm water (not too hot and not too cold) to assimilate to the temperature of your body, the effect is very detoxifying. Taken in the early morning, lemon water is a natural diuretic which encourages and supports the healthy function of the liver and kidneys and helps to flush out the nasties. In addition, it keeps the body and skin hydrated and if you sip it 10–15 minutes before breakfast, it will also help to kick start enzyme production in the gut and aid digestion.

Once ingested, the alkaline properties of lemons can really help to balance pH levels, regulate cholesterol, aid digestion and generally make the body more alkaline, allowing it to function at its optimum best. It is thought that consuming lemons may also help to fight organ deterioration and ageing, and help to resist the onset of arthritis and rheumatism.

Lemons are also high in Vitamin C, with each lemon providing about half the required daily intake, essential for the immune system and our cold-fighting abilities. Lemons also contain a boost to potassium and folate levels while lutein and zeaxanthin will help to keep eyes healthy. Lemons and limes do not not contain fat, sodium or cholesterol. However, they contain significant amounts of calcium, thiamin, niacin, Vitamin B6, phosphorus, magnesium and copper, all of which contribute to health and vitality.

Scurvy, a gruesome disease with symptoms including fatigue, extreme sensitivity and pain, purple skin spots, swollen gums and loose teeth, is often associated with sailors hundreds of years ago. It is caused by a deficiency of Vitamin C (which the body can only store for just three months) and is now incredibly rare due to the presence of fresh fruit and vegetables, most notably lemons, in modern diets. While James Lind, the Scottish doctor for the British Navy, first proved in the 1700s that citrus fruit protected against scurvy, he did not distinguish between lemons and limes, nor was he able to pinpoint the ingredient in citrus fruit that prevents scurvy. This led to many investigations and experiments and the eventual isolation of Vitamin C

or absorbic acid being credited to Albert Szent-Gyorgyi who was awarded the 1937 Nobel Prize in Physiology or Medicine for identification of Vitamin C. Such are its complexities that Haworth and Karrer also received the Nobel Prize that same year, this time in Chemistry, for determining the structure of Vitamin C.

Citrus fruits contain dozens of other useful chemicals, including lycopene, a molecule of the carotenoid family which is valued for reducing the risk of atherosclerosis and coronary heart disease.

With so many benefits to health and wellbeing, perhaps the humble lemon really is the 'Prince of Fruits'.

LEMON, FENNEL AND ROCKET SALAD WITH RADICCHIO

I AM PARTICULARLY FOND OF THIS SALAD. LEMONS GROW PROFUSELY IN THE SOUTH OF ITALY AND THEY'RE SWEET ENOUGH TO EAT OFF THE TREES!. I THINK A LEMON WILL IMPROVE THE FLAVOUR OF ANY DISH. I'M ALSO A BIG FAN OF RADICCHIO. MY FATHER WAS A MAJOR IMPORTER OF RADICCHIO WHICH IS GROWN IN AND AROUND VERONA.

- ½ radicchio (red chicory), the leaves torn into large shreds
- 2 large unwaxed lemons, peeled and finely sliced
- 1 fennel bulb, peeled and finely sliced
- a generous handful of rocket/ arugula, torn if the leaves are large
- 2 tablespoons extra virgin olive oil
- 2 tablespoons freshly grated Parmesan cheese
- a few drops of good balsamic vinegar
- sea salt and freshly ground black pepper

SERVES 4

Arrange the radicchio on 4 individual plates. Add the lemon slices, fennel and rocket/arugula.

To make the dressing, mix together the olive oil, Parmesan cheese and vinegar in a small bowl and season to taste with salt and pepper. Pour the dressing over the plated salad just before serving.

BUTTERNUT SQUASH WITH LIME DRESSING AND TOASTED SEEDS

BUTTERNUT SQUASH IS A QUICK AND SIMPLE VEGETABLE TO PREPARE AND EAT. THIS DISH WORKS WELL AS A LIGHT SNACK OR AS AN ACCOMPANIMENT TO PAN-FRIED CHICKEN OR SLICES OF GRILLED HALLOUMI CHEESE.

a 1-kg/2¼-lb. butternut squash, peeled and sliced into even-sized wedges (seeds reserved and rinsed)

3 tablespoons olive oil

a handful of sesame seeds

zest and juice of 2 limes

1 teaspoon fragrant clear honey

2 tablespoons fruity extra virgin olive oil

a handful of flat-leaf parsley leaves, roughly chopped

sea salt and freshly ground black pepper

a baking sheet lined with parchment paper

SERVES 4

Preheat the oven to 200°C (400°F) Gas 6.

Arrange the slices of squash on the prepared baking sheet and drizzle over the oil. Bake in the preheated oven for about 15 minutes, until tinged brown around the edges and the flesh is tender.

Meanwhile, put the sesame seeds and reserved butternut squash seeds (patted dry with paper towels) in a small frying pan/skillet set over a low heat (you will not need any oil). Toast until lightly browned.

Mix together the lime zest, lime juice, honey and fruity olive oil in a small bowl and season to taste with salt and pepper. Pour the dressing over the warm squash. Garnish with the parsley and toasted seeds and serve.

AUBERGINE WITH LIME NUT BUTTER

A MIDDLE EASTERN INSPIRED DISH THAT IS EQUALLY AS COLOURFUL AS IT IS NUTRITIOUS. NUT BUTTER IS EXCELLENT TO MAKE IN ADVANCE AND WILL STORE IN A JAR IN THE REFRIGERATOR FOR 1 MONTH.

250 g/2½ cups mixed shelled nuts, such as peanuts, almonds, walnuts, brazil nuts, cashews, hazelnuts, pecans and pistachios

2 teaspoons fragrant clear honey

4 teaspoons sea salt

2 medium aubergines/ eggplants

2 tablespoons olive oil

finely grated zest and juice of 2 unwaxed limes

a handful of fresh mint leaves, to garnish

1 medium red chilli/chile, de-seeded (if preferred) and finely chopped

a baking sheet lined with parchment paper

SERVES 4

Preheat the oven to 200°C (400°F) Gas 6.

Roughly chop the nuts and place them on the prepared baking sheet. Roast in the preheated oven for 3–5 minutes. Remove from the oven, tip into a bowl and stir through the honey and half of the salt. Tip back onto the tray, spread out and return to the oven for a further 5 minutes. Remove from the oven and set aside to cool.

Slice the aubergines/eggplants into thin rounds. Scatter with the remaining salt and place in a colander for 10 minutes. Rinse well and pat dry with paper towels.

Preheat a griddle pan until hot. Brush the dry aubergine/eggplant slices with oil and griddle until golden brown on both sides. Remove and arrange on a serving platter.

Blitz the roasted nuts with the lime zest and juice in a food processor until smooth.

Drizzle the aubergine/eggplant slices with the lime-nut butter and garnish with mint leaves and chilli/chile.

SWEETS
AND
DRINKS

La véritable
LIMONADE
1ᵉʳ CHOIX
GARANTIE
PUR SUCRE
L' Originale

LIME MARMALADE

AS EASY TO MAKE AS TO EAT.

6 small limes

3 unwaxed lemons

2 kg/9 cups granulated white sugar

3 sterilized jars (see page 4)

MAKES 3 X 450-G/1- LB. JARS

Scrub the limes and lemons, cut into quarters and remove the seeds. Fill a large pan with 3 litres/ 12 cups of water and soak the fruit for 24 hours.

Remove the fruit from the pan and cut into small shreds. Return to the water in which it has been soaking, bring to the boil and boil for 1 hour.

Next add all the sugar to the pan. Boil again until the juice forms a jelly when tested. To test if the marmalade is ready, place 2 teaspoons of the mixture on a cold saucer. Press the surface of the marmalade with your thumb and if it wrinkles, it is done. Let cool for 10 minutes.

Transfer the marmalade into sterilized jars and seal. Store in a dark, cool place. For the best taste, allow the marmalade to set for 1 month.

LEMON BANANA CURD

THIS SWEET, THICK SPREAD IS WONDERFUL ON BREAD, ICE CREAM OR PANCAKES.

4 large bananas

125 g/1⅛ sticks butter

250 g/1¼ cups caster/granulated sugar

grated rind and juice of 2 lemons

a pinch of ground ginger or 1 teaspoon chopped fresh ginger

4 eggs

2 sterilized jars (see page 4)

MAKES 2 X 450-G/1-LB. JARS

Peel the bananas, place in a bowl and mash with a fork.

Melt the butter in a saucepan, then add the sugar, bananas, lemon rind and juice and ginger. Cook gently over very low heat for 10 minutes.

Beat the eggs in a bowl, then gradually beat in 3 tablespoons of the banana mixture. Pour the egg mixture into the pan and continue stirring. Cook gently, stirring constantly, for 10 minutes or until mixture coats the back of a wooden spoon. Do not boil.

Pour into hot, sterilized jars and seal. Store in fridge and eat within 10 days.

LIMONCELLO GELATO IN BRIOCHE BUNS

DECADENT AND DIVINE, THIS INDULGENT TREAT IS SO ON-TREND AND
IS SERVED ALL OVER ITALY.

finely grated zest and juice
    from 3 unwaxed lemons

200 g/1¾ cups icing/
    confectioners' sugar

450 ml/scant 2 cups double/
    heavy cream

3 tablespoons Limoncello
    (see page 156), ice cold
    from the freezer

4 brioche buns, halved

SERVES 4

Put the lemon zest and juice in a large bowl. Stir in the sugar and
leave for 30 minutes.

Whip the cream with the Limoncello into soft peaks, then beat in
the lemon juice mixture. Pour into an ice cream machine and churn.
Alternatively, turn into a plastic tub, cover and freeze for 30 minutes,
forking the mixture halfway way through to prevent it freezing into
a solid block.

Serve the gelato scooped into brioche buns.

LEMON SYLLABUB

AN OLD FAVOURITE THAT NEVER FAILS TO MAKE A GOOD IMPRESSION.
SERVE CHILLED WITH DELICATE COOKIES.

finely grated zest and juice
    from 2 unwaxed lemons

100 g/½ cup golden caster/
    granulated sugar

250 ml/1 cup double/heavy
    cream

4 tablespoons dry sherry

SERVES 4

Put the grated zest and juice into a large mixing bowl. Add the sugar,
cream and sherry and whisk until thick and the mixture falls off your
spoon with ease.

Divide into 4 individual glasses and chill for 2 hours before serving.

LEMON PROFITEROLES

LEMONS ABOUND ON THE AMALFI COAST. I INVENTED THIS RECIPE FOR MY GRANDPA, BECAUSE HE LOVED PROFITEROLES AND HIS BUSINESS WAS GROWING LEMONS.

LEMON PASTRY CREAM
375 ml/1½ cups whole milk

½ vanilla pod/bean

3 large/extra large egg yolks

125 g/2 ¾ cups caster/
granulated sugar

45 g/½ cup Italian 'oo'
plain/all-purpose flour

finely grated zest of
2 unwaxed lemons

PROFITEROLES
125 g/1⅛ sticks unsalted
butter, cut into pieces, plus
extra for greasing

1 teaspoon caster/granulated
sugar

a pinch of sea salt

125 g/1¼ cups Italian 'oo'
plain/all-purpose flour

4 large/extra large eggs

TO SERVE
250 ml/1 cup double/heavy
cream

zest of 1 unwaxed lemon,
cut into thin strips

*2 large baking sheets,
buttered*

*1 piping/pastry bag,
fitted with a 1-cm/½-in.
plain nozzle/tip*

*1 piping/pastry bag,
fitted with a 5-mm/¼-in.
plain nozzle/tip*

SERVES 8

To make the lemon pastry cream, place the milk and the vanilla pod/bean in a medium saucepan. Heat over a medium-low heat until scalded (just up to boiling point). While the milk is heating, whisk together the egg yolks and sugar in a large bowl. Add the flour and stir until completely dissolved. Slowly whisk one-third of the scalded milk into the egg yolk mixture. Add the remaining milk all at once and blend thoroughly.

Pour the mixture back into the pan and return it to the heat. Stir until the pastry cream has thickened. Turn off the heat, add the zest and continue to stir for 1 minute. Remove the vanilla pod/bean. Pour the mixture into a bowl and place a piece of parchment paper on top to stop a skin forming.

Preheat the oven to 220°C (425°F) Gas 7.

To make the profiteroles, combine 250 ml/1 cup cold water, butter, sugar and a pinch of salt in a medium-heavy saucepan over a medium-low heat. As soon as the mixture reaches the boil, remove the pan from the heat.

Add all the flour at once and stir with a wooden spoon. When the flour is thoroughly blended in, return the pan to the heat. Stir vigorously for 1–2 minutes, or until the mixture pulls away from the sides of the pan, forming a ball of dough. Remove the pan from the heat and rest it on a damp kitchen cloth. Beat in the eggs, one at a time, incorporating each egg thoroughly before adding the next.

Spoon the profiterole mixture into the piping bag fitted with the larger nozzle/tip. Pipe 24 small mounds of dough 4 cm/1½ in. in diameter and spaced about 5 cm/2 in. apart on the baking sheets. Moisten your index finger with water and gently flatten the pointed peaks.

Place the baking sheets in the oven, staggered so that they are not on top of each other. Bake for 20 minutes, or until golden. Reverse the position of the baking sheets after 15 minutes so the profiteroles bake evenly. Turn off the oven and cool the profiteroles in the oven with the door ajar.

To serve, beat half the double/heavy cream until stiff. Stir this cream into the lemon pastry cream to lighten it, then spoon this mixture into the piping/pastry bag fitted with the smaller nozzle/tip. Make a small slit in the side of each profiterole and fill with the pastry cream. Stack the profiteroles on a large serving plate, sprinkle with lemon zest and serve immediately. Serve the remaining double/heavy cream separately.

MANGO AND LIME JELLIES

COLOURFUL, LIGHT AND DELICIOUS, A CLASSIC COMBINATION AFTER
A LARGE MEAL. SERVE WITH LIME RELISH AND CREAM IF REQUIRED

**2 large ripe mangoes, pitted,
peeled and roughly chopped**

**7 tablespoons caster/
granulated sugar**

**20 g leaf gelatine/4 x gelatin
sheets**

**5 tablespoons Muscat dessert
wine**

3 tablespoons lime juice

finely grated zest of 1 lime

TO SERVE

**zest of 1 lime, or thin lime slices
dried in a low oven**

**200 ml/scant 1 cup single/light
cream (optional)**

SERVES 4

Purée the mango flesh in a food processor with the sugar until smooth.

Place the purée in a medium saucepan and heat gently.

Soak the gelatine in plenty of cold water for 5 minutes. Drain and
squeeze the gelatine and place in the pan with the mango purée. Stir
until dissolved. Add 500 ml/generous 2 cups water, the dessert wine,
lime juice and zest.

Mix thoroughly, pour into tall glasses and chill for approximately
6 hours.

Serve decorated with extra lime zest and cream, if desired.

GIN AND TONIC CAKE

A MAGNIFICENT SPECIAL OCCASION CAKE, FOR ALL GIN-AND-TONIC
LOVERS. THE SUGARED FRUIT DECORATIONS CAN BE PREPARED UP TO
TWO DAYS IN ADVANCE.

415 g/3¾ sticks unsalted
  butter, diced and softened

660 g/3 cups plus
  5 tablespoons caster/
  granulated sugar

13 eggs

1½ tablespoons gin

1½ tablespoons tonic water

zest of 2 lemons

zest of 2 oranges

420 g/scant 3¼ cups 'oo'
  plain/all-purpose flour

1 tablespoon baking powder

1 quantity Gin and Tonic Syrup
  (see page 140)

1 quantity Lemon Icing (see
  page 141)

1 quantity Sugared Fruit (see
  page 141)

*1 x 25-cm/10-in. round cake pan and
1 x 17-cm/6½-in. round cake pan,
greased with unsalted butter and
floured*

SERVES 20

Preheat the oven to 180°C (350°F) Gas 4.

In a food processor, cream together the butter and sugar. Break the eggs
into a jug/pitcher and pour them into the food processor, through the
feed tube, with the processor running. Pour the contents of the processor
into a large mixing bowl.

Add the gin, tonic, zest, flour and baking powder to the mixing bowl and
stir well to combine. (If you have a large domestic food processor or
one with a strong motor, the dry ingredients and flavourings could be
incorporated in the food processor.)

Pour the mixture evenly into the prepared cake pans. Bake the large
cake in the preheated oven for 50–60 minutes and the smaller cake for
40 minutes, or until a skewer inserted into the middle comes out clean.

Leave the cakes in the pans for 10 minutes.

Pour the gin and tonic syrup over the warm cakes, spreading it with
a pastry brush to ensure an even coating. Leave the cakes to cool
in the pans before removing.

Cut the tops off the cakes to make them level and even in height. Place
the larger cake on a serving plate and centre the smaller cake on top.

Pour the lemon icing over the top cake and let it drizzle down onto the
lower cake. Using a metal spatula, spread the icing to form a thin layer.
Let the icing dry for at least an hour before decorating.

Place the sugared fruits and leaves decoratively on the top cake and
around the edge of the lower cake.

GIN AND TONIC SYRUP

180 ml/$\frac{3}{4}$ cup gin
$3\frac{1}{2}$ tablespoons tonic water
250 g/$1\frac{1}{4}$ cups granulated sugar
zest of 2 unwaxed lemons

Place all the ingredients in a small saucepan. Stir over a low heat until all the sugar has dissolved and then bring to the boil. Boil gently for approximately 5 minutes, until a syrupy consistency is achieved.

LEMON ICING

380 g/2¾ cups icing/
  confectioner's sugar

1½ teaspoons lemon zest

70 ml/⅓ cup lemon juice

4 teaspoons extra light olive oil

In a small bowl combine all the ingredients and whisk until smooth.

SUGARED FRUIT

THESE PRETTY FRUITS CAN BE MADE UP TO TWO DAYS IN ADVANCE,
AND ADD THE PERFECT FINISHING FLOURISH TO YOUR CAKE.

a selection of small fresh fruits
  with skin (e.g. kumquats,
  grapes, figs, redcurrants,
  blackcurrants)

a few small kumquat, lemon
  or orange leaves or small
  grape leaves

1 egg white

200 g/1 cup caster/superfine
  sugar

To make the sugared fruit, wash and thoroughly dry all the fruits and leaves.

Pour the egg white into a small bowl and whisk it lightly.

Using a pastry brush, brush the fruits and leaves with egg white. Shake off any excess. Thoroughly sprinkle the fruits and leaves with the sugar, making sure they have an even coating.

Set the fruit aside on a dry tray or plate at room temperature for at least 2 hours, or overnight, before using. Do not refrigerate.

MESKOUTA
MOROCCAN YOGURT CAKE

THIS WONDERFULLY MOIST YOGURT CAKE IS SO EASY TO PREPARE –
I ENJOY WATCHING MY DAUGHTER DEVOUR IT AFTER A BUSY DAY AT
SCHOOL. FEEL FREE TO USE LIME ZEST INSTEAD OF LEMON IF YOU WISH.

4 large eggs, separated

120 g/¼ cup natural/plain yogurt

110 g/11 tablespoons vegetable oil (I use groundnut/peanut oil)

220 g/1 cup plus 1 heaping tablespoon caster/granulated sugar

needles from 2 sprigs of fresh rosemary, finely chopped

finely grated zest of 2 unwaxed lemons

2 teaspoons vanilla extract

330 g/2½ cups 'oo' plain/all-purpose flour

4 teaspoons baking powder

½ teaspoon sea salt

icing/confectioners' sugar, to serve

a bundt pan or ring mould, greased with unsalted butter and floured

SERVES 8-10

Preheat the oven to 180°C (350°F) Gas 4.

Beat the egg whites in a large bowl until stiff.

In a separate large bowl beat together the yogurt, oil, sugar and egg yolks with the rosemary and lemon zest. Stir in the vanilla, flour, baking powder and salt. Beat until smooth.

Fold in the egg whites carefully and incorporate evenly.

Pour the batter into the prepared bundt pan and bake in the preheated oven for 35 minutes.

Remove from the oven and allow the cake to cool in the pan before inverting onto a wire cooling rack. Let cool completely.

When completely cool, sift the icing/confectioners' sugar on top and serve.

LIME AND MINT GRANITA

THIS ICE-COLD GRANITA COULDN'T BE MORE REFRESHING. SERVE
ON A WARM SUMMER'S DAY. BEST ENJOYED AL FRESCO.

150 g/¾ cup granulated
sugar

grated zest of 2 limes

100 ml/scant ½ cup freshly
squeezed lime juice

90 g/4½ cups fresh mint
(I like to use apple mint)

lime slices, to serve

SERVES 8

Pour 600 ml/2½ cups cold water into a small saucepan, add the sugar
and lime zest and bring the mixture to a simmer. Cook, stirring, until
the sugar has dissolved.

Add half the mint (there's no need to chop or remove stalks) to the
saucepan, then take it off the heat. Cover with a lid and allow to
stand for 10 minutes, then remove the lid and let the mixture cool to
room temperature.

Once cool, strain the mixture through a sieve/strainer into a large jug/
pitcher, pressing firmly on the mint to extract all the flavour. Stir the lime
juice into the mint syrup and then pour into an airtight lidded freezer
container, 30 x 15 cm/12 x 6 in.

Place the granita in the freezer, then check it after 1 hour. Once it begins
to freeze around the edges, take a fork and stir the mixture, breaking up
the frozen parts near the edges into smaller chunks and raking them
towards the centre.

Return the container to the freezer, then check the mixture every
30 minutes, stirring each time and breaking up any large chunks into
small pieces with a fork, until you have fine crystals of granita. If at any
time the granita freezes too hard, simply leave it out at room temperature
for a few minutes until it softens enough to be stirred again with a fork,
and rake it back into crystals. Then return it to the freezer.

Serve in small glasses decorated with the remaining extra sprigs of mint
and lime slices.

PERUVIAN KEY LIME PIE

THIS IS MY VERSION OF THIS CLASSIC PIE, AND AS CLOSE
AS I CAN GET TO THE ORIGINAL RECIPE.

12 oat cookies, approximately
300 g/11 oz. (I often use
chocolate-covered ones)

150 g/1 ¼ sticks unsalted
butter, melted

2 large/extra-large egg yolks

397 g/1 ¾ cups condensed
milk

1 teaspoon sea salt

finely grated zest and juice
of 4 unwaxed limes, plus
1 extra lime for garnish

250 ml/1 cup double/heavy
cream

*a 23-cm/9-in. loose-based
tart pan*

SERVES 6–8

Preheat the oven to 160°C (325°F) Gas 3.

Crush the cookies to a fine crumb and mix with the melted butter.
Turn into the tart pan and press evenly up the sides and base. Chill
in the refrigerator for 30 minutes.

Once chilled, transfer the pie to the preheated oven and bake for
12 minutes. Cool on a wire rack.

Place the egg yolks in a large bowl and mix well. Add the condensed
milk and continue mixing. Add the salt, lime zest and juice and mix
thoroughly. Pour into the cooled base and bake for 20 minutes.

Cover and chill for at least 4 hours. To serve, whip the cream and
pile on top of the lime filling, then sprinkle with extra lime zest.

LEMON CARDAMOM AND RASPBERRY TORTE

FURTHER PROOF THAT FLOURLESS CAKES ARE DIVINE. BLUEBERRIES WORK AS WELL AS RASPBERRIES HERE. I SERVE THIS CAKE AT THE END OF DINNER PARTIES WITH DESSERT WINE.

125 g/1⅛ sticks unsalted butter, plus extra for greasing

200 g/1 cup golden caster/granulated sugar

10 cardamom pods, seeds crushed

finely grated zest of 1 unwaxed lemon

2 teaspoons vanilla extract

3 large/extra-large eggs

200 g/1 cup raspberries or blueberries

250 g/1½ cups ground almonds

a pinch of salt

1 teaspoon baking powder (gluten-free)

LEMON DRIZZLE ICING

200 g/1½ cups icing/confectioners' sugar

zest and juice of 1 small lemon

handful of toasted hazelnuts, finely chopped

a 23-cm/9-in. springform cake pan, greased and lined

SERVES 6-8

Preheat the oven to 170°C (325°F) Gas 3.

Cream together the butter, sugar, cardamom seeds, lemon zest and vanilla extract until pale and fluffy. Add the eggs one at a time and beat between each addition.

Fold in the fruit, ground almonds, salt and baking powder. When everything is mixed together, fill the cake pan with the mixture and bake in the preheated oven for 45 minutes until golden, and a skewer inserted into the centre comes out cleanly. Cool on a wire rack and then unmould.

To make the lemon drizzle icing, mix the lemon zest and juice with the icing/confectioner's sugar. Pour over the cooled cake and sprinkle with toasted hazelnuts.

THE SCIENCE OF CITRUS

LEMONS AND LIMES SHOULD BE CONSIDERED AS SIBLINGS OF THE CITRUS FAMILY AND ARE INDISPENSIBLE INGREDIENTS IN ANY KITCHEN, BUT THERE ARE SUBTLE DIFFERENCES IN THE WAY THEY SEASON A DISH.

Their appeal is the characteristically tasty, undoubtedly fragrant and highly appetizing qualities they can add to a dish and our palates. The differences between the two fruits are subtle, with limes being green and small and lemons being yellow and bigger in size.

They are two of the most acidic citrus and are generally not eaten on their own, with the exception of the sweeter variety of Meyer lemons which can be eaten fresh. They are both sweet and sour, simple and complex, and the uses for lemons and limes, much like the plants themselves, are seemingly endless and widely varied. While they are both acidic, limes have a higher acidity and lower sugar content, meaning that lemons are generally sweeter.

Lemons can find their way into almost anything in the kitchen, from recipes for ice creams, cakes, jams and tarts to shellfish platters and roasted chickens. The juice can be used as a replacement for vinegar in salad dressings and to add a kick to mayonnaise, and in their preserved state (see page 101) they are found in tagines, stews, soups, and rices and grains.

Lemons also have a useful household role as a natural cleaning agent and can be found in many perfumes. Interestingly limonene, derived from the lemon and present in the peel, is the primary ingredient for making menthol, the main source of mint flavour.

Limes are smaller, sharper and more intense. They are best used with spicy and exotic flavours, often to balance the heat of chilli/chile or garlic, and are an integral part of Indian cuisine. Limes are valued for the acidity of their juice and the aroma of their zest and are commonly used in authentic Mexican, Vietnamese and Thai dishes. Their pickling properties are widely acknowledged and are specifically called for in ceviche (a South American dish of raw fish marinated in lime juice, with the acid in the juice 'cooking' the fish). The most popular varieties include Kaffir, Key, Persian and dried or black limes, which are typically found in Persian and Iraqi cuisine and in the baharat and kabsa spice mixes. Limes are also used in dressings and garnishes, cocktails (particularly the Mexican margarita and Brazilian caipirinha), marmalades and desserts, most famously in Key Lime Pie.

Whatever the use, lemons and limes bring flavours alive by changing acidity. Of course the whole fruit can be used, but slices make a bigger impact than the juice or zest alone. A squeeze of fresh juice, however, cuts through other flavours and elevates a dish to a different level. Use lemon or lime juice with caution alongside dairy products, as too much will cause a sauce to curdle (after all, adding an acidic element to milk is the starting point for much cheese making!).

Both lemons and limes can also enhance flavours, much as salt does. In some recipes they can replace sugar while in others, perhaps best known in the cases of lemonade or limeade, they are added to sugar.

Lemons and limes have a cleansing effect on the palate and depending on whether they are used in their raw, cooked or preserved state, or whole, juiced or zested, the effects can vary hugely. It is wise to leave zesting until the last minute to prevent the oils from disappearing. Also note that lemons and limes work well combined with sweeter vinegars and marinades. While fresh juice can transform a pan sauce, avoid risking discolouration and introducing bitter tones by removing the pan from the heat and adding the juice at the end of the cooking process.

SALTY LIME SODA

I AM EXTREMELY FORTUNATE TO WORK AT MISTLEY KITCHEN IN MANNINGTREE. IT IS A BEAUTIFUL COOKING SCHOOL, SHOP AND RESTAURANT, RUN BY SHERRI SINGLETON, A LADY WITH A GREAT EYE WHO IS A VERY PASSIONATE COOK AND TRAVELLER. WHEN I MENTIONED THIS BOOK, SHE HAD NOT LONG RETURNED FROM A TRIP TO INDIA WHERE SHE ENJOYED THIS THIRST-QUENCHING DRINK MANY TIMES IN THE SWELTERING HEAT.

4 teaspoons good-quality
    sea salt
zest and juice of 4 limes
400-ml/14-oz. bottle of soda
    water
plenty of ice, to serve
lime slices, to serve

SERVES 2

Mix together the salt, lime zest and juice and soda water in a jug/pitcher. Pour into long tall glasses, and serve with ice and lime.

LEMON AND GINGER BARLEY WATER

THIS IS OH SO GOOD FOR YOU. BARLEY CAN HELP EASE URINARY AND CIRCULATORY PROBLEMS. GINGER IS FULL OF THERAPEUTIC PROPERTIES ALSO.

125 g/^{2}/$_3$ cup pot barley
zest and juice of 4 unwaxed
    lemons
100 g/^{1}/$_2$ cup brown sugar
5-cm/2-in. piece of fresh ginger,
    peeled and roughly grated
ice, to serve
lime slices, to serve

SERVES 4

Wash the barley and place in a large heatproof jug/pitcher with the lemon zest, sugar and ginger. Pour 1.2 litres/5 cups boiling water over the mixture and allow to cool for several hours.

When the mixture is cold, add the juice of the lemons. Strain and then serve in a glass with a little ice.

SUNDAY MOJITO

MY HUSBAND AND I FIRST ENJOYED THIS MOJITO ON OUR HONEYMOON IN THE TROPICS.

1 lime, cut into eight
4 lychees
6 sprigs of fresh mint
6 tablespoons Malibu
2 tablespoons lychee liqueur
ice, to serve
2 tablespoons pineapple juice

SERVES 2

Place the lime into a cocktail shaker. Using a muddle, crush the lime with the lychees and mint. Add the Malibu, lychee liqueur and plenty of ice. Shake vigorously. Strain into cocktail glasses, top with pineapple juice.

PALOMA

A SECRET PASSION OF MINE. ONLY ONE MIND YOU, IT WILL MAKE YOUR TONGUE WAG!

100 ml/scant ½ cup tequila
150 ml/⅔ cup pink grapefruit juice
4 teaspoons fresh lime juice
2 teaspoons vanilla sugar
ice, to serve
lime and grapefruit wedges, to garnish

SERVES 2

Add the tequila, fruit juices and sugar to a shaker with ice cubes and shake. Strain into highball glasses filled with ice cubes. Garnish with lime and grapefruit wedges.

FERRIGNO FAMILY APERITIF

THIS IS A WONDERFUL ICE-BREAKING COCKTAIL WHICH MY GRANDFATHER INSISTED ON SERVING AT ALL FAMILY GATHERINGS.

2 tablespoons Limoncello (see page 156)
Prosecco
ice, to serve
a slice of lemon
a sprig of fresh mint

SERVES 1

Pour the Limoncello into a large wine glass and top up with Prosecco. Add the ice, lemon slice and mint. Serve at once.

LEMON-LIME SYRUP

DELICIOUS POURED OVER HOMEMADE GELATO, USED IN COCKTAILS OR CAKES, OR SIMPLY SERVED WITH SPARKLING WATER. THIS SYRUP ALSO MAKES A WONDERFUL GIFT.

zest and juice of 4 unwaxed
    lemons

zest and juice of 2 unwaxed
    limes

450 g/2¼ cups golden
    caster/granulated sugar

75-cl/25-oz. bottle, sterilized (see page 4)

MAKES 750 ML/3 CUPS

Pour the lemon and lime juice into a saucepan, add the zests, sugar and 100 ml/7 tablespoons water. Bring to the boil, then turn off the heat and let it rest overnight.

Strain the syrup through a muslin. Pour the syrup back into the pan and bring it back to the boil for 3 minutes, then pour it into the sterilized bottle.

To serve, allow 1 measure of syrup to 5 measures of water. Keeps for up to 1 month in the refrigerator.

LIMONCELLO

THIS LIQUEUR IS MADE THROUGHOUT SOUTHERN ITALY. IT IS GOOD AFTER A MEAL IF YOU LIKE THE SWEETNESS, AND SOME ITALIANS LOVE IT POURED OVER THEIR GELATO.

6 unwaxed lemons

75-cl/25-fl. oz. bottle of vodka
    (or pure alcohol)

225 g/1 cup plus 2 tablespoons
    caster/granulated sugar

450 ml/16 fl. oz. pure bottled
    water

75-cl/25-oz. wide-necked sterilized jar (see page 4)

SERVES 6

Put the lemons in a bowl of cold water and leave to soak for 1 hour. Remove from the water and dry with paper towels.

Using a vegetable peeler, carefully peel the rind from the lemons, taking care not to remove the white pith.

Put the lemon rind in the sterilized jar. Pour over the vodka and seal the jar. Leave in a cool, dark place for 20 days.

After 20 days, put the sugar and the bottled water in a saucepan and bring to the boil, stirring to dissolve the sugar. Remove from the heat, cover and leave until cold.

When cold, add the sugar mixture to the lemon zest mixture. Strain the mixture, pour into a sterilized bottle and seal. Leave in a cold, dark place for a week before serving.

Serve cold and, once opened, store in the refrigerator.

INDEX

ACKNOWLEDGMENTS

Thank you to Cindy Richards, for suggesting that I write this book. Thank you for your confidence in me, it has been such a pleasure yet again. Julia Charles, thank you again and again. The subject matter of this book has been thrilling, I have loved cooking and re-testing and learning so much along the way. Without your dedication and determination this book would not shine. Thank you for your humour and your keen eye to produce beautiful books that matter. Miriam Catley, I enjoyed our marathon edit and thank you for noticing every little detail. Clare Winfield, thank you for your stunning work your light touch in both senses of the meaning is a gift. Sonya Nathoo, your enthusiasm for your subject is so clearly evident through your magnificent design of this book – gorgeous to meet you and thank you so much. Emily Jonzen and Matthew Ford – fabulous work, thank you for keeping the dishes real. Jo Harris thank you for the super enhancing props.

Thank you to my daughter, Antonia, and my husband, Richard, for sampling my dishes along the way, with honesty and thoughtful critisim that was most necessary. Sally Daniels my super duper friend and trusted transcriber, I value your speed and professionalism more and more, you are incredible.

PICTURE CREDITS